Easy Self-Discipline

How to Resist Temptations, Build Good Habits, and Achieve Your Goals WITHOUT Willpower or Mental Toughness

Easy Self-Discipline

James W. Williams

PUBLISHED BY: James W. Williams

© Copyright 2021 - All rights reserved.

The content contained within this book may not be reproduced, duplicated or transmitted without direct written permission from the author or the publisher.

Under no circumstances will any blame or legal responsibility be held against the publisher, or author, for any damages, reparation, or monetary loss due to the information contained within this book. Either directly or indirectly.

Legal Notice:

This book is copyright protected. This book is only for personal use. You cannot amend, distribute, sell, use, quote or paraphrase any part, or the content within this book, without the consent of the author or publisher.

Disclaimer Notice:

Please note the information contained within this document is for educational and entertainment purposes only. All effort has been executed to present accurate, up to date, and reliable, complete information. No warranties of any kind are declared or implied. Readers acknowledge that the author is not engaging in the rendering of legal, financial, medical or professional advice. The content within this book has been derived from various sources. Please consult a licensed professional before attempting any techniques outlined in this book.

By reading this document, the reader agrees that under no circumstances is the author responsible for any losses, direct or indirect, which are incurred as a result of the use of information contained within this document, including, but not limited to, — errors, omissions, or inaccuracies.

Table of Contents

2 FREE Gifts 1

Introduction 5

   How to Use This Book 11

Chapter One - Why Change? The Importance of Habits Over Self Discipline 14

   Why Cut Bad Habits and Develop New Ones? 16

   The Science Behind Habits 23

Chapter Two - Take The Leap: Getting Started on Your Journey 26

   How Your Habits Fulfill Your Needs 29

   How Your Habits Control Your Life 32

   Cue > Craving > Response > Reward 33

   The Myths of Habit Change 40

Chapter Three - How to Become the Person You Want to Be 45

   Identifying Who You Want to Become 47

Chapter Four - How to Let Go of Your Bad Habits & Form New Ones 54

   Identifying Your Habit Cues 56

   Understanding Your Habit Cues 61

   Taking Control of Your Habit Cues 67

   Mastering the Cue's Existence 69

Mastering the Cue's Appeal 71

Mastering the Cue's Difficulty 74

Mastering the Cue's Satisfaction 76

Chapter Five - Creating the Perfect Environment for Success 81

Change Your Environment. Change Your Life 85

Chapter Six - Making Your New Habits Effortless 92

You Only Need to Master Showing Up 93

How to Do Things Even When It's Hard 98

How to Involve Other People for Greater Success 100

Chapter Seven - The Importance of Habit Tracking 110

The Benefits of Habit Tracking 111

Tips for Integrating Habit Tracking Strategies into Your Life 118

The Best Habit Tracking Strategies You Can Use Today 122

Chapter Eight - The Power of Reflection 138

The Dark Side of Forming Positive Habits 139

Final Thoughts 148

References 151

James W. Williams

2 FREE Gifts

To help you along your personal growth journey, I've created 2 FREE bonus books that will help you master your mind, become more confident, and eliminate intrusive thoughts.

You can get instant access by signing up to my email newsletter below.

On top of the 2 free books, you will also receive weekly tips along with free book giveaways, discounts, and more.

All of these bonuses are 100% free with no strings attached. You don't need to provide any personal information except your email address.

To get your bonus, go to:
https://theartofmastery.com/confidence/

Free Bonus Book #1: *Master Your Mind: 11 Mental Hacks to Eliminate Negative Thoughts, Improve Your Emotional Intelligence, and End Procrastination*

Discover the techniques and strategies backed by scientific and psychological studies that dive into why your mind is preventing you from achieving success in life and how to fix them.

You will learn how to:

- Deal with stress, fear, and anxiety
- Become more emotionally intelligent

- Communicate better in your relationships
- Overcome any and all limiting beliefs you have
- Avoid procrastinating
- Actually enjoy doing difficult tasks
- And so much more!

Free Bonus Book #2: *Bulletproof Confidence Checklist: Eliminate Limiting Beliefs, Overcome Shyness and Social Anxiety, and Achieve Your Goals*

In this book you will discover how to overcome the limiting beliefs that results in lack of confidence and social anxiety.

You will learn practical tips to rewire your negative thought patterns, break free from shyness, and become the best version of yourself.

Introduction

I was 24 years old when I decided it was time to change my life. And when I say change my life, I mean to sort it out entirely. I remember that night like it was yesterday.

It was winter, and I had not long moved back into my parents' home after me and my girlfriend at the time had split up. It was two in the morning as I went outside to the front porch, lighting a cigarette the moment the door closed behind me. It was the last cigarette in the packet— my last savior. My mental health had not been great the last few months, and even though I didn't have a lot going on in my life, I felt stressed and depressed most of the time. I told myself that these little moments were my moments of escape.

What's more, since my parents lived in such a rural area and I had always been driving my ex-girlfriend's car, getting to the stores was more than a hassle, not that any around there would be open around that time. I had to make this one count.

The outside light flashed on, and snow crunched under my feet. I didn't know it had been snowing, so I hadn't worn a coat. I just stood in the wind with my shirt wrapped around me tightly. Something caught my eye. I don't know what it was, but it caused me to turn sharply, so sharply I dropped the cigarette into the wet slush by my feet. I panicked. I picked it up as quick as I could, as though that was going to stop it from getting wet, and brought it back to my lips, where it hung as limp as a boiled piece of spaghetti. My attempts to light it were in vain. At first, I was angry. My last one. I was stressed. I felt myself become tense while clenching my fists and gritting my teeth. I felt so much frustration over something so small I wanted to scream. I'm not the sort of person to want to punch a wall, but the thought certainly crossed my mind. I felt such an extreme amount of disappointment.

Then something happened. I let go. I felt complete disbelief that I had actually become so wound up and angry over something so small. Was I really that irritated at something like not being able to have a cigarette? Did such a horrible habit have that much control over me? Something clicked. It was as though my life over the last few years, ever since being in school as a teenager, a young adult in college, and now a 20-something in the world of work, all flashed before my eyes. I saw where I was. I saw how I was living my life.

Going to the fridge and eating any junk food I could find instead of making proper, somewhat substantial meals. Smoking. Never really exercising. Watching porn daily (sometimes multiple times a day). Sitting for hours in front of the TV every night after work, not doing a whole lot else. All these things I did in my life without really thinking about it. Things that just kind of happened. There was no thought or intention behind them. I just did it. I was living my life on autopilot. It was depressing, to say the least.

Where was my life going? What direction could I take? I realized that it could take any direction I wanted to take. I could become anyone and do anything. I could write books or start businesses. I could become someone. I felt sadness expressed on my face. How could I do all those amazing things when I can't even do the basics like looking after myself? Maybe I could find out?

And so, my journey into habits and self-development began.

I believe that human beings have incredible potential to do amazing things in their lifetime. You included. We both really do live in a world where anything is possible, and we all have the opportunities to do whatever we want to do. Yet, on a fundamental level, so many people lock themselves into what others refer to as "the rut." I've spent years of my life there. You probably have too.

Since you're reading this book right now, you know there are already aspects of your life that you want to change. You know there are things you do that are bad for you, perhaps even killing you, and are actively stopping you from becoming and being the person that you actually want to be. You're aware that there's something in your life that's stopping you from moving forward. Old habits you can't let go of. Past behaviors you try to change, yet, for some reason, no matter how hard you try, you always seem to end up back where you were.

You're not alone. There are millions of people in the same situation.

There are several happiness-based studies out there that monitor how happy people are in countries worldwide, the most prominent being the World Happiness report. People are asked how happy they are (as well as census information about their lifestyle like income and so on) on a scale of one to ten. The vast, very vast majority of countries rank about five on the scale. So right in the middle. The US ranks as the 18th country on the index with a rating of six. At least it's over halfway, but there's certainly room for improvement.

A question: Do you see yourself as two people?

For me, there was always the person I am now, and then the person I wanted to become. It was always some future version that could happen one day, perhaps. But do you wonder how you'll get from here to there? Are you stuck trying to figure out how to make the transition on what can sometimes feel like some impossible feat?

Do you live your life wishing you'll cocoon up like a caterpillar and miraculously transform into the beautiful butterfly version of yourself overnight? Is there some deep-down part of you that believes that's never going to happen? You've tried so many times before, but you're still stuck here. It can feel nothing short of depressing.

Hands up if you've gotten into bed one night after a bad day and vowed to yourself that tomorrow, you're going to wake up, and everything's going to be different. Tomorrow, you're going to make all those wonderful changes you want to make in your life, and you're going to become the person you've always dreamed of being. How many times have you had that conversation with yourself? How often have you woken up and made an effort, but the "new you" lasts a couple of days max before you slip back into your old ways and find yourself spinning around this loop again and again and again?

You're not alone in this way of thinking. I've been there. I still sometimes go there. I've seen so many people in my life beat themselves up because they can't seem to find a way to break their mold. It seems there's some impossible barrier holding them in place. They can't seem to escape the confines of their old, habitual selves and blossom into the beautiful version of themselves they know it's possible to be.

Yet, it is possible. Very possible. Entirely possible.

It's so possible that you can start making the necessary changes right here, right now. The results of which can, and probably will, last an entire lifetime. It all starts with habits.

Your habits. Those little actions you do each and every day, most of which you do without thinking. These little actions are the core of who you are and define you as an individual, and if you don't have control of these, you're a slave to your own biology. But hey, let's not get carried away and dive straight into the deep end. Instead, let's explore what this is all about.

Positive change with long-lasting effects. What we're exploring through this book is how you can master your habits and become that person you want to be. A person who knows and sticks to their values and heads in the direction they want to head when they want to head there. It's a path I'm walking and am now taking you along for the ride.

What's more, I used to believe that I needed to conjure up some insane amount of willpower and discipline to stick to my guns. Turns out I needed none. All I needed was innovative thinking, a feasible approach, and a mission.

This is my guide to help you do the same. This is my guide to creating long-lasting, beneficial habits with easy self-discipline that actually works.

How to Use This Book

The book in your hand is an accumulation of journal entries, notes, both successful and failed attempts, and recordings I've made over the years when it comes to my self-development journey, coupled with the teachings of some of the best-selling and most acclaimed writers, researchers, and habit experts to grace the modern age, and mentions of the scientific and psychological research that backs it all up.

Throughout the following chapters, I'm going to dive into what it means to develop healthy habits, exploring why it's something you should be thinking about bringing into your day-to-day life and how you can immensely benefit from taking yourself off autopilot and taking control of how you live your life. I was going to use a "grasp the joystick" metaphor, but that seemed a bit far.

We'll start by getting on the same page about what habits actually are and how they work so we know what we're aiming for, and then we're going to explore how you can make it happen. Know now, there is nothing in this book that suggests you're going to need to reach down deep within yourself and pull out some immense amount of willpower to force yourself to stop following through with your bad habits. You won't need to meditate cross-legged on your living room floor while surrounding yourself with your favorite foods, snacks, and addictive pleasures as an attempt to change your ways and rewire your brain.

That's not to say we won't be doing some casual brain rewiring because we certainly will, but this guide is all about making your process easy, effortless, and pain-free. Importantly, I want you to have fun. I will try and make this as fun as possible, but it's up to you to see this journey as an adventure. Up until now, I bet you've seen the process of changing your habits as something that you need to do. A chore of kinds. A necessity. Switch this out right now.

Try viewing this approach as an adventure. This book has washed up on the shore of your desert island; you've opened the pages and found a map. Where the X lies, there's the version of yourself that you want to become and the life you want to live. Here's under the X where you've made your dreams come true. However, there's a lot of quests and adventuring to do first, so strap up your bootstraps, push your raft out onto the waves, and let's do this the easy way because Lord only knows you've done this the hard way for far too long.

While you can read this book however you want, I highly recommend this. Read the entire book from start to finish. Don't necessarily stop and start working on one aspect. Read the whole thing and then reflect on what parts stood out to you. Your journey may currently be in a certain place where you need a specific approach, but you're at another stage for other habits in your life.

For example, one habit you might be trying to stick at, and it's really not working, and you keep giving up time and time again. As a result, you lack motivation, which is why you'll need to work on identifying why you're trying to focus on that habit while seeking clarity for your efforts.

On the other hand, you might have a habit that's coming on really well, so well that you're looking at taking it to the next stage. If this is the case, you may really benefit from the presence of an accountability buddy. See how your needs are different?

Again, read the book from start to finish, then reflect and figure out what you need. I'll recommend strategies for various stages of the process as we go to help you have some ideas, but you'll be able to feel what's right and what isn't.

This isn't a book that's all about telling you strictly how to do things, although you could certainly treat it that way if that's what you think you need. Instead, this book is about educating you with the knowledge you need to make the best decisions for yourself, both now and at any other stage of your life.

Are you ready for the adventure of a lifetime?

Without further ado, let's begin the journey.

Chapter One - Why Change? The Importance of Habits Over Self Discipline

"We are what we repeatedly do. Excellence, then, is not an act, but a habit." – Aristotle

Back in 2018, Will Smith posted a viral clip on his Instagram page where he shared the quote that "Self-discipline is self-love."

Ever since I saw that clip, the message has stuck with me. He goes on to describe that if someone in your life was struggling with something, say they're trying to break an old habit, trying to exercise more, eat healthily, be more social, and so on, then you'd happily give them the advice to help them. Of course you would. You'd want your friend to make the right choices because you want them to be happy, healthy, and living the life they want to live. You want them to make the right decisions because you love them.

Let's say you want to lose weight. If a friend comes up to you and says, "I'm thinking I want to lose weight," you would say something like, "Well, you're going to need to exercise and eat healthy foods." You'd maybe offer to go to the gym with them, so it's not so daunting, or you may even go on a diet with them, so they're not feeling so lonely about it. You could probably come up with a million suggestions for ways they could fulfill their goals.

Yet, when it comes to your own life and your own habits, you seem to fail time and time again to make the right choices. "Right" being defined as the decision we actually want to make. In this example, but applied to you, you could say you want to eat healthily and lose weight, and you could give yourself the same advice that you'd give your friend, but the chances that you'll actually follow it through are pretty slim.

About ten years ago, I suffered from intense social anxiety, so much so I became addicted to video games because it gave me an escape and somewhat fulfilled a social need. It got to the point where I played such a ridiculous number of hours a day, yet I still kept going.

I knew that playing video games for eight hours a day was bad for me, insanely unproductive, unhealthy, and was holding me back. If a friend were going through the same thing, I would have advised them to stop. Yet, because it was me and I was only talking to myself, I found myself falling back into the same trap over and over again. The longer I stayed in the rut, the harder and harder it became to escape.

In the words of Will Smith, I know what's good and bad for me, and not having the self-discipline to make the right decisions was a clear sign that I didn't love myself.

If I did, then I'd surely be treating myself right. So, I tried it. I tried to brute force myself to stop playing games and to get my act together—the same with smoking. When I decided to quit, I threw away the cigarettes I had and went cold turkey.

For years, I went through the same cycle of sticking with my new habit for a few days, maybe a week at a push, before finding myself back exactly where I started and indulging in these bad habits once more. Only this time, there was the added weight of guilt, shame, and failure resting on my shoulders.

I believe that Will Smith is on to something. To show self-discipline is to love ourselves, but this is the message, not the solution.

You can't brute force your way into a new life. The solution instead starts with the reason why.

Why Cut Bad Habits and Develop New Ones?

Going back to the chapter title, why change?

Some reasons for changing your life are simple. You want to be fitter and healthier so you can do more and have more energy. For me, I wanted to write books to help people and "change the world" (I know, it's cliche, but hey, we all need a dream). Some people want to buy the house of their dreams, start a family, grow a business, travel the world, and so on.

Deep down, we all have dreams and aspirations we want to fulfill, but making those dreams become a reality is something few people know how to achieve. After all, if we did, we'd be doing it already. I want to let you in on a bit of a secret. So how do you get there into the position where you're doing it? The answer to this should be no surprise and is by far the most important lesson I've learned on my journey of self-improvement.

Your habits. Your habits define you.

The macro decisions you make each and every day are the decisions that will guide your life in the direction it goes. There are few big life-changing moments in anybody's life, but there is an infinite number of small moments where real change happens. Whether you're conscious of it or not, these micro-decisions are who you are.

Use my smoking habit as an example. If I say I'm quitting smoking and am no longer a smoker, these are words, not actions. If I go to a bar with friends later that evening and all my friends are smoking, there is a moment, a singular moment, where the craving hits, and I either ask my friend if I can have one, or I don't.

It's a time frame of less than a second, but it's that tiny moment where I'm either a smoker or I'm not.

Depending on the decision I make right then, it will impact me for the rest of my life one way or another. It's kind of mind-blowing, isn't it? How many times have you gone to do something on your phone and somehow, without recollection, you're 15 minutes into an Instagram scrolling session, and you don't even know how you got there? This is because picking up your phone and scrolling is so hardwired into you. It's automatic. It's a habit. Yet, that scrolling time is time you're never ever ever getting back.

Imagine if it was easy to put on your running shoes and jog three times a week. Or sit down and write five pages of the book you've always wanted to write each and every day and have it finished within a few months. Imagine being able to work on that business idea or have the time to spend quality time with your partner or work on your college essays. Imagine that world. Isn't that where you want to be? That version of you that finds it effortless to do what's right?

It all starts with habits.

The idea of habits, and the very definition of it, is to do something so automatically, it takes no effort and no thinking. Merriam Webster defines it as an action or behavior that is reinforced by repetition. Something you do automatically over and over again.

Your brain LOVES these. Every single second of your life, your brain is analyzing your surroundings and your environment. It's checking out what's going on, and it's making decisions that aim to keep you healthy and alive. However, it always strives to complete these neural processes in the simplest and most energy-efficient way possible. The less brainpower being used, the more brainpower you have to work on other, more complicated tasks that may arise.

Studies published by *Science Daily* claim that around 40 percent of our daily lives are made up of just mindlessly habitual routines and habits, many of which are so automatic, you don't even know you're doing them.

Basically, your brain is a supercomputer that's trying to automate life as much as possible. However, our brains also haven't really changed that much from an evolutionary standpoint in hundreds of thousands of years, yet our external environment has changed infinitely. We live in a hyperstimulating world where we're constantly bombarded with content and images and sex, food, cars, and dreams.

Everything is available at the click of a button and is made easier and more accessible for our own convenience. This evolution of "stuff" is literally playing on the trait that our brain wants things to be easy. This is why it's so easy to pick up your phone and scroll. It takes no effort, and the feedback is instant. When you go into a dark room, you automatically turn on the light switch. Your brain is hardwired to do it automatically.

Yet, in the hyperstimulating world, we find ourselves hardwiring the super easy stuff like eating junk food, scrolling, binging Netflix, and disregarding the stuff we actually want to do. In his groundbreaking habits book *Atomic Habits,* James Clear writes how binging Netflix is so easy because literally all we have to focus on is keeping our eyes open, hence why auto-play is a feature. How insane is that realization?

By taking control of these micro-decisions and making the harder, more challenging, more fulfilling dreams you want to fulfill as easy as binging Netflix, you can take your life in the direction you want to go and live the life you want to live. But don't just take my word for it. Here are some of the scientific benefits to taking control of your habits:

- Your habits are you. If you say you're a vegan, but you eat meat, you're not a vegan. The actions you take every day are who you are as a person, so taking control of this means you take control of who you are.

- You can reach your goals. By making conscious decisions in your life, you can set out to reach your goals and do the things you want to do, no matter what these things are. It's all about taking steps in the right direction while minimizing the risk of spending time doing things that don't matter to you, like procrastinating.

- You look after yourself. Working on developing good habits usually means you start looking after yourself in all other areas of your life. This means you'll be healthier, more active, more social, stronger, and more productive.

- You improve your mental health. Torturing yourself with bad habits and feeling the shame and guilt that you can't seem to stop feeling doesn't have a good effect on your mental health. Developing healthy habits allows you to shed these weighty feelings and has been proven to help reduce and even overcome depression, stress, and anxiety.

- You stop wasting time. You, like me, spend so much time doing things that mean nothing. I'm not saying it's not good to have downtime and rest, nor that relaxing and enjoying a movie is a bad thing. Far from it. But not knowing your plan, not having aims, and sitting on your phone for four hours every day scrolling are not bringing any benefit to your life.

- You don't need motivation. If you want to brute force a healthy habit into your life, it requires motivation, discipline, and willpower, and if you have a bad day where you don't feel like doing something, you need endless motivation that, let's face it, is never going to happen. When something is so automatic, you don't even need to think about it. You don't need motivation. You just do it.

- You help those around you. Looking after yourself and making conscious decisions doesn't just benefit you, but it also helps you better connect with the other people in your life and inspires them to make better decisions.

You see me talking a lot about how the art of developing good habits revolves around the idea of making conscious decisions. This is the crux of this book. Whenever you're faced with a decision, you have a choice to make, and it's in these split-second moments that make you who you are. This book is about making those decision-making moments automatic in favor of what you want, rather than automatically doing the thing you're already programmed to do, which might not be what you want.

It's going to take a bit of work, a bit of mindfulness, and some changes to your life, but it's entirely something you can start integrating. With that, I think it's pretty clear why developing good habits is a good idea and why it's something you should be focusing on.

The Science Behind Habits

Of course, if you've read any of my other books, then you know I love stats, data, and science, and while a large part of the habit-forming "process" is subjective to the individual, the neural and psychological science behind habits is not. It's all very proven and well-researched stuff.

Habits are formed unknowingly for the most part, and they are carried out automatically for the majority of people. Habits enable us to do the hundreds of tasks we need and wish to complete in our lives. It frees up our thinking processes to work on other things because we can carry out a habit without having to think about it. But where did it all begin?

Well, with nothing less than a drop of saliva.

If you have any interest in psychology, you've probably heard of Ivan Pavlov. A Noble Prize Winner in Medicine, Pavlov mainly worked with dogs to study the digestive system. However, when researching digestion, he came upon something that startled him.

Pavlov was observing the amount of saliva produced by dogs during digesting. He first noted that dogs salivated when they saw food, even before tasting it. Then he observed that if the meal was associated with another event, like a bell or the experimenter's footsteps, the dog would eventually start salivating at the simple sound of the bell or even footsteps. This is what we now refer to as classical conditioning.

There is a link between two things that cause a habit to come together. In this case, there is a "cue," or a stimulus, which is the food, and a reaction or response, which is salivating.

The cue (meal) causes a response (salivating)

After that, you can add in a new cue. In this example, the response occurs when Cue 1 (food) is combined with Cue 2 (bell) (salivating).

Over time, you'll be able to delete the original cue (food) and have the response elicited solely by the next cue (bell):

The cue (bell) causes a response (salivating).

You're probably wondering what this has to do with you at this point. You probably don't want the habit of drooling every time you hear a bell ringing. Imagine that world.

It's this pattern of cause and effect that creates habits. Now, a lot of research has been done on habits over the years because they make up the majority of our lives.

We're going to break this structure down and look at it in detail in the following chapters, but for now, it's just important to start understanding how habits work and what kind of habits you have in your life. Remember, this journey is all about you and finding out what works for you in your own way, so keep thinking about how all these points tie into your own circumstances.

Chapter Summary

- Habits are the small actions and behaviors you do in your life over and over again
- The more you practice a habit, the more mindlessly and automatically you'll be able to do it
- Your brain LOVES habits because they make life easy
- We live in a world where effortless habits are encouraged, but mainly for the wrong reasons
- You can create your own new habits to control the direction your life is heading
- You can take control right now

Chapter Two - Take The Leap: Getting Started on Your Journey

"If you're brave enough to say goodbye, life will reward you with a new hello." — Paulo Coehlo

This chapter is going to be a short chapter that basically ties together everything you've learned so far and sets the scene for the journey you're about to start. From here on out, it's quick-fire tips, actionable advice, and all the knowledge you'll need to set up your systems and make them work. There's no going back from here, not that you'd want to, but it's where you'll start to see real change happening.

Let's make sure we're on the same page.

There's an extremely slim chance you'll ever be able to wake up one day, snap your fingers, and you'll be a different person. Your mind, brain, and everything about you and every other human on the planet are just too stuck in its ways. That's literally how we're designed to be. That's what we call "the comfort zone."

Instead, we're going to be focusing on making lots of little changes over a long period of time. As James Clear explains, if you were to get 1 percent better at something every day for a year, come the end of the 365-day period, you'll be a full 37 times better than you were when you started. Thirty-seven times? That's a huge gain by only getting better at something a little bit each day.

This is what habit experts refer to as "results compounding," which works in the same way as compound interest in finances. You make small gains that build up and get better and bigger over time. You could put $250 in a savings account one month and keep it there. However, since you need to pay bills and so on, you can't do this consistently every month, so the habit of saving money never forms. On the other hand, you could save $40 a month from your paycheck, and you'd have saved $480 at the end of a year. Since you've consistently paid it in, the money is there waiting for you, and you'll have created the habit of saving every month.

Instead of $250 a year in odd savings that creates $2,500 in savings over the course of a decade, you'll have consistently saved $5,760. It's a big difference.

Whether it's habits or finances, this adventure is all about making a little bit of progress consistently rather than trying to achieve bulk, lump-sum results. However, it's this very notion that stops you from being successful. It's a bit of a double-edged sword.

Whenever you set out to do something, you want to see the results that your time is worthwhile. This is especially the case since we've been conditioned to live in a world of instant gratification.

You upload a photo on Instagram, you instantly get likes. You buy a lottery card, and you can see if you've won in seconds. You want to eat something nice, you get a snack out of the fridge. You want to buy something new, Amazon will deliver it the next day.

If you want to get fit, you can't see results from the gym after one session. If you want to write a book, it's not going to be good after one day. You can't learn a new language in a few hours.

This is the first obstacle you're going to need to learn to overcome.

Whenever humans try to do something in life, the vast majority of us focus on the outcome as the end goal. You want to learn French so you can speak French. You want to go to the gym because you want to be fitter. There's a massive gap in this way of thinking because the process doesn't work like that. You can't put the effort in at once and expect to be at the end goal. This is why you fail to develop a new habit over and over again. You expect a reward for your actions that doesn't come, at least not immediately.

You don't see the results, so you believe you're wasting your time and give up, falling back into your old habits.

And what are your old habits? They are desires to fulfill a need.

How Your Habits Fulfill Your Needs

When you really think about it, the habits you're thinking about changing in your life are simply short-term solutions to your long-term problems. And these short-term solutions are only fulfilling your basic human needs.

You eat because you're hungry. You play video games and binge TV because you want to be entertained or not bored. You watch porn because you're lonely. You smoke because you're stressed. There are plenty of long-term solutions for all of these needs that do need to be fulfilled. You could meditate or journal to release the stress in your life, but you need to do it for a considerable amount of time to acquire the benefits from these practices.

Smoking, on the other hand, fulfills the need instantly. The truth is that you don't actually want to smoke. Millions of people smoke, fully aware of the negative health implications of what it does. This is only because the health problems compound over the long term, much in the same way the positive ones can. You have one cigarette or miss exercise for one day, you're not going to get lung cancer or become overweight.

However, consistently fulfilling these habits creates a problem. Just like getting 1 percent better every day leads to a 37x improvement over a year, getting 1 percent worse every day will lead to you being in a place 37x worse than you are now.

But even without the facts of why smoking is bad, you don't actually want to smoke. All you want to do as a human being is fulfill your need not to be stressed and fulfill it as soon as possible.

So, you're going about your day-to-day life, and you start feeling stressed. Someone says something or something happens, and it gets to you. This isn't the first time you've been in this position, so your brain says, "Hey, we have a need to fulfill! I'm stressed! What can we do to feel better?"

Your mind then goes back into your past and says, "Well, last time we had a cigarette or we ordered a takeaway, and that made us feel better straight away. Let's do it again!"

So you order a takeaway and spark up. Every time you make a decision like this, you're voting in favor of that action being the one you take and ultimately will form a habit around. The more you do it, the more your brain sees this as the way to do things. Thus, a habit is formed.

This raises a fundamental question: How do you mix things up and form a new habit? If your brain is simply taking care of and fulfilling your needs, and it already votes for the bad habit to fulfill it automatically, how could you possibly go against your own brain's hardwiring? I'm sure there are habits you've had for decades. How do you overcome them?

The simple answer is to vote for change in the opposite direction, but you already know this isn't going to work. It's an approach like that where you would need discipline and willpower. Instead, you need a change of mindset, or rather a change in what you're focusing on.

When you want to learn a new language, you might find yourself watching YouTube videos of cats rolling around in the sand because it's easy. The whole concept of being fluent in French sounds fantastic, but it's so difficult and will surely take years of practice. *I'll start one day when I have time,* you may say to yourself.

However, to switch things up, the basis of this new strategy is to forget the long-term plan and instead focus on something I like to call "winning the moment."

Winning the moment is not about focusing on the long-term goals of learning a language, quitting smoking, or being fitter and healthier, but rather winning the split seconds you have when you're faced with making a decision. This is why I said the crux of this book is all about making conscious decisions.

That means there's no willpower needed. No discipline. No motivation. Just the act of making a different decision when it matters most.

Of course, writing it this way makes it sound easy. It's not. There is always a bit of work to do, but it's also not as hard as you may think it is. When it comes down to it, the habits you practice hardly revolve around decision-making at all but around the systems that control your life that lead up to those decisions. But we'll get into that in a second.

For now, bear in mind that a change in perspective and some extra attention in some areas of your life is what you need, and it's certainly easier than trying to force change and mix up your life in one big, dramatic attempt.

How Your Habits Control Your Life

Before we move forward, it's crucial you understand how habits work. We've discussed the science behind the psychology, but let's explore it in real terms that are actually applicable to you. You can't change what you don't know. There's a ton of research that has gone into this, but no matter what you're reading, the main foundation concept for how habits work is the process known as "the habit loop," which looks a little something like this (we'll explore some examples afterward):

Cue > Craving > Response > Reward

Cue - There is always a cue that kickstarts the habit loop. The cue is the trigger that makes you want to do something. This could be internal or external and sends a signal to your brain for it to do something.

Craving - Your brain has had a need triggered by the cue, and you develop a craving to take action. You want or need something to satisfy the need that has been triggered.

Response - You take action. We've been talking about conscious decision-making, and this is the stage where they are made. You do something to fix your craving.

Reward - You take action, and it has an instant result. Your brain remembers the rewarding feeling as being a good thing or a bad thing, so next time the cue comes up, it knows what to do; hence, the loop is formed.

The more you cycle through the same loop, the more set the habit becomes in your life.

This was proven to be the neurological way the brain works in a recent MIT study. The study took rats and placed them in a T-shaped maze. When they reached the intersection, a tone was played that cued the rat to go left or right. If they chose correctly, they were given a reward.

Once the researchers were happy the rats had the tones down as a habit, they stopped rewarding the rats, but they still continued to run the maze correctly. Even when they spiked the rewards with light chloride that induces nausea, the rats continued to follow their trained habits.

When given brain scans, they could see that specific regions of the brain had hardwired in the program of hearing the tone and going in a particular direction for a reward.

Here are some common, basic examples of how this cycle works.

Cue	**Craving**	**Response**	**Reward**
Your phone pings with a notification.	You want to see what the notification is.	You check your phone.	You get a rush of dopamine because someone liked your photo, sent

			you a message, or commented on something.
Your mouth feels dirty.	You want a clean mouth.	You brush your teeth.	You feel good because your mouth is clean, and you feel confident because your breath smells nice.
You're bored.	You want to be entertained.	You watch TV, play video games, masturbate, eat junk food.	You feel good that you're no longer bored and have been entertained.
You hear a	You want	You turn	Your

sound.	the reward for turning in the right direction.	left or right.	curiosity is satisfied.
You're feeling stressed and irritable.	You want to feel calm and stress-free.	You smoke a cigarette.	You feel calmer and less stressed.

These are some pretty standard habits that most of us have, but you can see how it gets complicated when you start looking into the intricacies of your life. If your habit loop looks like the last entry, then it's a habit that's doing you way more harm than good. However, you're fulfilling a need, which is why you stick with it.

When it comes to redesigning your life and developing positive habits, the trick is to break the cycle of this loop and instead replace your existing loop with one that you consciously want. Remember what we said about you not actually wanting to smoke or eat junk food, but you're fulfilling a need? This is where a lot of people fail.

Up until this point, I bet your mindset is all about quitting smoking or cutting lousy food out of your life. You want to spend less time on your phone and be more social. The problem is that you're never actually breaking the habit loop, which is why you constantly find yourself back at square one. You're telling yourself that you're never going to take action when you feel a craving, but then you're leaving the need unfulfilled.

Your brain reaches this kind of dead-end where it needs to do something to fulfill the need, and it only knows how to do it in the way you've always done it, which is why the craving starts to feel more intense until eventually, you cave, relapse, and find yourself back where you were.

This strategy is not about giving anything up. It's not about quitting anything or cutting anything out of your life. You're not giving anything up. It's about choosing another option. It's about creating a habit loop that you actually want to have and have control over while reducing the chances that you'll fall into the old habit loop entirely. If you can do this well (which this book will teach you), you won't need the existing habit loops that you feel are holding you back because you'll have new ones you want in their place.

This is what effective habit-forming is all about.

Fortunately, you can redesign a habit by switching the initial stages of the habit loop. In an ideal world, this means if you wanted to stop binge eating every time you felt stressed, we would be aiming to ensure you never feel stressed, and therefore don't binge eat. Of course, that's not going to happen, but there are ways around it. Exciting stuff, right?

There's a lot to cover, but as the exercise to finish off this chapter, I want you to grab a pen and paper, or even the Notes app on your phone, and write down all the things in your life you want to change or areas you want to grow. List out all the bad habits and things you do that you don't like doing but can't seem to escape from.

List them out and next to them, start filling in the habit loop variables. This is a widespread practice when it comes to habit setting, especially among high performers. It's a great place to start when it comes to understanding yourself and finding out where you're at right now.

Your table may look a little something like this:

Cue	Craving	Response	Reward
I feel bored/lonely.	I want to distract myself.	I check my phone.	I feel distracted.

I feel sad.	I want to feel happy.	I eat junk food.	I feel better.
I hear my phone notification ping.	I want to know what the notification is.	I check my phone.	I get a little rush of dopamine seeing the notification.
I feel lonely.	I want affection and attention.	I watch porn and masturbate.	I feel slightly better for a short period of time.

All the habits you'll list will probably end up in the responses column, so I recommend you start here and then work out what your cravings and cues are. This is such an interesting part of the process because, perhaps even for the first time, you'll start to really zero in on what makes you do what you do and what kind of life you're living.

You might not be able to do this all in one sitting, so take notes as you go through your day and notice things. Just build up a list and your understanding of yourself before moving ahead to the next stage of your journey.

The Myths of Habit Change

There are certainly some myths out there that you'll need to think about regarding habit change and some mindset shifts that undoubtedly hold people back. Indeed, the biggest and most prominent is that you need an insane amount of willpower and self-discipline to become who you want to become. The sooner you can let the notion go, the sooner you can move forward with your efforts.

Willpower is a Myth, Self-Discipline is a Lie

Willpower is a myth.

You don't need motivation to change your habits. That's not to say you don't need something to inspire you to want to do better, but there are endless people who believe that you need some kind of superhuman level of self-discipline to become the person you want to become.

That's a lie. It's all a lie. We've spoken a bit already about how habits run on your brain's neural pathways. In the very literal sense, your habits are hardwired into you. This is why it takes such a tremendous amount of willpower to hold back and to change. It's why it simply doesn't work as a long-term strategy.

Let's say you're a smoker and you're trying to quit smoking since this is a straightforward example. You say you're going to quit, and everything is going fine until *bam!* You get stressed, and the neural pathway in your brain lights up, saying it's time to have a cigarette in response to feeling this way to help you unwind. When you're using willpower and self-discipline, you'll try and resist the craving.

You take a few deep breaths, try talking to someone around you, and you're able to take your mind off it eventually. Later, you go to work, and you smell cigarettes in the street and *bam!* You're triggered once more, and you find yourself fighting that urge.

You could potentially encounter hundreds of these cues in a single day, and there's literally no human on Earth with enough willpower or discipline to literally fight their mind that many times throughout the entire day. This is why you're constantly fighting a losing battle when you take this approach to habit change.

You can never simply brute force your way to a new life.

This is why I'm writing this book. This is why all the habit gurus and experts of the research field try to get their messages out to the masses. You need to have a plan when it comes to habit mastery. You need to have a strategy in place. You don't need impossible human levels of discipline or willpower. You need to make the changes as easy as humanly possible, so you're setting yourself up for the most minimal chances of failure. This is why you need to place your efforts on creating systems, not just using up your limited reserve of willpower.

Sure, self-discipline is a part of it because you need it to start off making your plan, and there are going to be times where it's hard. No journey is perfect, but willpower and discipline are not the be-all and end-all. Willpower, in this sense, is a tiny part of the journey.

It's about living smarter, not harder.

I Don't Want to Be a Slave to Routine

This is a common question I hear all the time when talking about habits. People say something along the lines of "I don't want to be a slave to my routine. If I wake up every day and I'm just doing the same thing day in, day out, life will get so boring and so stale. I won't truly be free."

This is wrong on so many levels. Plain and simple. Firstly, if you see habits in this way, then you're already a slave to the way you're living your life. Every cigarette, every TV show you watch, every junk meal you eat when you get sad, and so on is a habit that you do without thinking. With that mindset, you're a slave to it, even more so because you're doing most of these things without thought.

When someone who says they're going to stop watching porn inevitably finds themselves getting into bed at night and loading up their preferred website without even so much as a second thought, when reality hits, they're hit with guilt and shame, feelings that leave a real strain on the body.

Setting up good habits is all about setting you free. When you can optimize and routine the core elements of your life where you're looking after yourself and putting your health, well-being, and productivity first, you're then free to explore any other paths in life. This is where you'll find true freedom.

Say you want to write a book, as I did for many years. Instead of thinking creatively and taking the time to sit down and actually write a book, I would spend each and every day battling with the fact I was smoking, or looking up how I could eat healthily but with minimal effort, or beating myself up because I didn't think I was socializing enough or getting enough exercise. This way of living and thinking is habitual in itself, and it's not going to help in any way when it comes to doing the things you actually want to do.

Instead, if you can master the basics of your life and, in a sense, get the fundamentals of your life down to a tee, so much so that you don't even need to think about doing what's best each and every day, then you're truly putting yourself in a place where you can experience freedom in a way you've never experienced it before.

Chapter Summary

- Your habits exist to fulfill a need.//
- The reason you can't change your habits is because you aren't fulfilling the need. You're only taking away your vice.
- Your life runs on macro-behaviors that form habit loops.
- You can change your life by taking control of your habit loops and creating your own.
- Many of us only ever focus on the response part of a habit without ever addressing the rest: the causes, the cues, or the cravings.

Chapter Three - How to Become the Person You Want to Be

"Let go of who you think you need to be and just be who you actually are." – Anonymous

If you're reading this book, then the chances are that you've tried again and again to change the habits in your life but failed. I guess that's the case, anyway. It's how I was for many years. It's a horrible feeling because you feel like a failure and can't seem to grasp why you're going around and around the loop of trying to be better but being unable to do it. It's crushing for your self-confidence, but it's still possible to make things right.

Throughout the last chapter, you've gone through the process of taking stock of where you are now and how your current habits are influencing your life.

This is where we start to see where the problems lie.

For so many years, whenever I attempted to address a bad habit, I would always use the same language and the same approach. Do any of these sound familiar?

- Tomorrow I will stop going to bed late
- I will stop eating unhealthy food

- I'm not going to watch porn anymore
- I won't play video games so much
- I will stop binging Netflix all weekend
- I will not drink so much alcohol

All of these are good habits to break, but do you see the similarity in the statements? You're saying to yourself, I'm going to stop doing XYZ, and then you're just hoping for the best that it's going to happen. There are so many things wrong with this. The statements, or technically goals, are too vague. There's no plan of action. There's such a negative connotation to what you're doing, and of course, this will put you off. This is why you always fall back into your old ways of living.

Remember what we spoke about a few chapters ago? Every habit you have is designed to fulfill a need. Whether that's to stop being bored, fulfill a basic desire, deal with your emotions, or whatever it is, your habits exist for a reason. To simply say I'm not going to do that anymore is not enough because you're going to leave that need unfulfilled. With nothing to take its place, this is why you end up back where you started or relapsing, as it were.

When you consider that a habit is simply an action or a response that has temporarily fixed a need in the past, you're bound to feel really uncomfortable when you give it up because your brain has been hardwired to know that there is a fix available, and will wonder why you're not doing it. In essence, you're fighting against your own neurology.

Instead, you need a plan. You need to take action. You need to approach your new habits with a strategy for success, not just to draw a line and say enough is enough. Here's how.

Identifying Who You Want to Become

To start with, you can't become the person you want to be, the best version of yourself, if you don't know what you want. You've probably thought about this a lot in different ways, but now is the time to bring it all together. Start by writing down the person you want to be. Just quick-fire notes of whatever comes to mind. Usually, this list will consist of the bad habits you're trying to change but framed in the opposite way.

A list could look something like this:

- I get up at 6 a.m.
- I will be sociable three times a week
- I will eat healthy food
- I will exercise regularly

- I will read books
- I will save more money

These are great, and I'm sure even reading some of these points, you're nodding to yourself and thinking, *Yeah, even if I could do at least some of these things. I think I'd be happier, healthier, and more stable in various areas of my life.* Perhaps you have a dream you're trying to pursue, like writing a book or starting a business. You could then list things like "I want to write every day" or "I will work on my business idea for five hours per week."

These are all great ideas, and you should see how even reframing the language here is so much more beneficial. Instead of saying "I will cut out junk food," which makes it feel like you're cutting something out of your life and depriving yourself of being able to fulfill your needs, you're giving yourself an alternative, to a degree.

I say to a degree because these sentences are not enough to change your thinking or rewire your brain to break the bad habits. If you're feeling sad and want to eat junk food, but you've told yourself you want to eat healthily, your brain will still say, "Hey, junk food worked. I'm not giving that up." Hence, you go back to junk food.

However, they are the foundation of where the real change starts and will help to guide you in the right direction.

At this point, you just want to think about what kind of habits you want to work on. The fact that you've picked this book up in the first place probably means you have some ideas, but really take time to think about it or rewire once you commit to a particular habit. You're going to want to stick with it consistently and build up momentum. In other words, you want to make sure you're focusing on the right elements of your life.

If you're unsure of what habits you want to introduce, here are some pointers to get you started, habits where you can't really go wrong.

Get Active and Exercising

Sure, you've heard this all before, but exercising, even just a little bit each day, like doing a couple of stretches here and there, is going to be beneficial to you and your overall health, well-being, and happiness.

Exercise has been proven to improve your self-esteem and boost your confidence. These are benefits that will affect every single area of your life. Exercise also reinforces the habit of positive thinking because you're looking after yourself and showing yourself a degree of self-love. You're also giving your energy to do more with your days.

You also get the benefits of lower stress and tension that allows you to think, resulting in improved mental well-being in your life as a whole. Some studies show that exercise can boost creativity levels and ways of thinking.

Focus on One Thing

If you develop the habit of only doing one thing at a time and minimizing how much you multitask, you'll be opening your life up to a far more beneficial and satisfying way of living. You'll be more productive and get more done with your duties. It's been proven repeatedly that it's so difficult to accomplish critical goals if you're continuously switching projects and becoming distracted by other "vital" matters.

You'll be less stressed overall and happier throughout the day.

Minimizing Your Life

Get rid of anything that isn't absolutely necessary. It's literally that simple. By having stuff in your home and space that you don't actually want or need, you're cluttering yourself and your mind, and it's just not a peaceful way to live life.

Instead, determine what is most essential in your life—the most important things to you and those you enjoy the most. After that, get rid of everything else.

This simplifies things and allows you to focus on what matters most. This method may be applied to any situation, including your personal life, work projects and assignments, email, and other forms of communication.

This is a great way to transform your life because it enables you to simplify, focus on what matters most, and create the life you desire. You can make this a habit by regularly going through your things and sorting them in this way.

Being a Generous Person

Because why not create a habit of being kind?

If you focus on becoming a generous person every day for a month, you will notice significant improvements in your life, both in terms of how you feel about yourself and how connected with other people you are. Over time, you'll notice that others react to you differently and treat you better. If you believe in karma, this one's for you.

To begin, aim to do something nice for someone every day, even if it's something small. Decide on that good deed at the start of the day, and then carry it out throughout the day.

You can also try to be kind, polite, and compassionate every time you interact with someone.

So, whether you've got your own ideas of things you'd like to work on, or feeling inspired from some of the ideas above, let's have a quick recap and see where we're at.

You know that your existing habits exist to fulfill a need in your life, a process that is reinforced over time by the repeated habit loops in your life. Some of these habit loops provide you with short-term rewards over long-term gain, and these are the bad habits you'd like to break.

What's more, using the previous exercise, you've identified what kind of positive habits you would like to have to replace the bad ones. So, that begs two questions:

How do I give up my bad habits?

How do I start practicing the good ones?

And as a side note, there really is no such thing as a good habit or a bad habit. There are only ever habits you want and habits you don't want. In some aspects of your life, you'll be happy doing what you're doing. When you're young and free, you'll like going to a bar for a few drinks, meeting friends, and having a good time, but if you get older and you're at the bar all the time and not doing much else, nor looking after yourself, then it becomes a problem.

What's good and bad for you will change as you go through life, meaning that this entire process of habit mastery is ongoing.

And with that, we go back to our questions.

How do I break my bad habits?

How do I start practicing the good ones?

In the following chapters, we're going to dive into the habit loop we were talking about in the previous chapter and identify how you can become a master of your own. This way, you'll be able to stop carrying out your bad habits and start implementing new ones. Take another look at the habit loop.

Cue > Craving > Response > Reward

We'll start with the first step.

Chapter Four - How to Let Go of Your Bad Habits & Form New Ones

"The only proper way to eliminate bad habits is to replace them with good ones." - Jerome Hines

At this point, you'll have some idea of the habit loops that make up your life, for better or for worse, and you'll have some idea of which direction you want to go as you move through this habit mastery journey. Your brain is doing these loops constantly every second of every day. Even as I write this, I'm sitting in front of my computer with my Word document open (cue). I want to finish this chapter, so I get the craving to write. My response is to write, which gives me a hit of dopamine when I've finished this sentence.

I then move on to this paragraph, and I'm starting again. Then I'm just doing this over and over. Now I look outside and see it's a lovely sunny day. I hear the birds singing and see the sun shining. This is a trigger cue that gives me the craving that I want to go outside. My response is to take a break and go for a walk around my local park. My reward is that I get to enjoy the nice weather and all the physical and mental benefits that come from going for a walk.

On the other hand, I get writer's block, and I feel sad (cue). Because I don't want to feel sad, I get the craving to pick up my phone and scroll through Instagram to distract myself. My response is to pick up my phone and scroll, and the reward is that I'm distracted from my sad feelings. While on Instagram, I see a photo of a pretty model, and this sexually arouses me (cue). This triggers the craving to watch porn and masturbate (response), and I satisfy that need.

See how this event is just a series of habit loops following on from each other one after another? That pattern makes up the building blocks of life. That's what the entirety of human behavior is made up of. Now, the more often I repeat these processes, the deeper and most consistently these habits form. Over time, whenever I get writer's block, instead of sitting down and dealing with it, I end up watching porn and distracting myself because this is what I've always done, and it works to a degree. Of course, in the long term, it doesn't, but in the short term, I'm distracted and not frustrated at myself anymore.

As this process continues, every time I feel sad, I want to distract myself by masturbating, and ultimately this can turn into a sex or porn addiction (a bad habit). It's the same with smoking, eating, drugs, alcohol, TV binges, and so on. All those little crutches we have in life are short-term answers to problems we have used in the past and, for that moment, they worked.

So, how do we break the habit and form a new one? In this first section, we're talking about redefining your cues.

Identifying Your Habit Cues

Your habit cues can come from anywhere, and there are so many potential variables.

To start with, it's impossible to control all of your habit cues. That should go without saying. You're never not going to feel sad, which could trigger the craving to eat that cake or binge Netflix, nor is there never going to be a time where you're not feeling lonely, which could trigger the want to swipe through Tinder. We'll talk more about how to deal with these issues in a bit.

On the other hand, there are plenty of cues you can control and start sorting out right here, right now.

For example, do you have a bad habit of checking your phone at all hours of the day? Many believe it's somewhat sad we've reached a point where so many of us actually feel a pang of panic when we touch our pockets and realize our phone is not where we thought it was. Perhaps you've caught yourself in the act of reaching out for your phone for literally no reason, only to question why you had such an instinctive act.

It's no secret that many of us are living with some kind of phone addiction, even if it's mild. While there's no denying this technology can do amazing things that help us day to day, it also provides a major distraction that can hold you up.

Looking at the stats, 77 percent of Americans have a smartphone (and there are around 3.5 billion smartphone users globally), and the average number of times a phone is checked by each user is around 56 times (more than twice per hour), with excessive cases, especially among teens and young adults, clocking in about 160 times per day.

That's time you pick up your phone and unlock it to check notifications or to carry out a task. Timewise, Americans spend an average of 5.4 hours per day on their devices, which clocks in at a jaw-dropping 37 hours a week. That's like waking up at midnight Monday morning and then solidly using your phone until Tuesday afternoon without a break. Imagine how much more you could do in that time.

If you're unsure of your own usage, I highly recommend using a tracking app like the built-in Screen Time function on iOS or downloading an app from the app store. I did this for a month, and I was shocked with my own stats and how much time I was using it.

Anyway, pulling this back around to having healthy habits, the smartphone is an excellent example because the devices themselves are designed to create various cues and cravings specifically to play on the habit loops. They grab your attention and draw you in, using them over and over again, all based on the same psychology. Most commonly, if you're to receive a text or notification, the audio ping and visual lighting up of your phone triggers the habit cycle.

Cue	Craving	Response	Reward
You hear your phone ping.	You want to see what it is.	You check the Instagram notification.	You get a dopamine hit that you got a like on your cat photo.

Because you fulfilled the habit loop and got a minor dopamine hit at the end, your brain says, "Hey, we just did a good thing," and reinforces that the habit loop was a beneficial thing to do. Next time your phone pings, the same cycle happens again, solidifying it was the right thing to do, and it continues endlessly.

Start at the beginning—the cue. By removing or at least reducing the cue, you break the habit loop because you're preventing it from triggering you in the first place. In this specific example, there are multiple ways to do this.

- Keep your phone in another room while you're working
- Turn the phone to silent mode
- Change your settings to stop notifications from appearing
- Use Do Not Disturb mode
- Delete the apps you don't want to be distracted by

This same logic applies to every other habit in your life. If you want to eat healthily, don't buy unhealthy food that's going to sit in your eyeline every time you open the fridge. If you live in a family household, simply putting the junk food at the back of the fridge behind healthy food can be a good enough action in itself to stop you from picking at it.

Easy Self-Discipline

If you play too many video games, disconnecting your games console and putting it in the cupboard where you can't see it can be enough to stop you from playing on it. Even walking into a room and seeing your Playstation can send the cue to your brain to start playing and induces that craving.

Modern televisions play on this because they now offer a main menu feature, rather than going to a specific channel where you have to scroll. You turn the TV on (because you're not easily hiding this away in any room), and there's the Netflix logo. Then the habit loop begins.

Cue	Craving	Response	Reward
You're bored.	You want to stop being bored.	You see the TV and the Netflix icon and click on it.	You get a dopamine hit because you're not bored anymore.

Go through your list of existing habits and figure out where your cues are and what triggers you. If you're feeling bored, you might automatically head to the TV, the fridge, or the cigarettes. Once you start paying attention to this area of your life, you'll be amazed at just how much of an impact your cues have on your life.

Understanding Your Habit Cues

More often than not, the cues in your life don't come from specific events happening in your life but rather come from environmental cues and general lifestyle situations.

For example, every morning I wake up, I play on my phone. I go to my office and check my emails. I then set up whatever project I'm going to be working on that day. I go downstairs and make a coffee, then I go back to my office and start work. This is literally the same routine I do every day, so it's safe to say it's a habit. It's a habitual routine.

What's my cue for this loop of habits? Is it my environment? Am I working? Somewhat. The cue here is even simpler than that.

It's the time of day.

Time is such a massive cue in our lives that it's so easy to overlook and mostly is. Even waking up in the morning begins a stream of habits like brushing our teeth, showering, having breakfast, getting dressed, and so on. The cue of waking up triggers the entire series of events, much of which we do without even thinking.

Easy Self-Discipline

Many of your habits will follow suit. Perhaps you have a break at work every day at 10 a.m., which is why when it gets closer to that time, you start craving a cigarette or coffee, even when you're not at work itself. If you get bored and always snack at 3 p.m., you'll find you do this every day.

Cue	Craving	Response	Reward
It's 3 p.m.	You want a snack.	You eat a snack.	You feel good because you fulfilled a need.

Then when it gets to 3 p.m. the next day, your brain remembers you had a snack and felt good, so it remembers that was a good thing to do and triggers the cue at 3 p.m. to have a snack. Hand in hand with this line of thought, location is another primary habit cue.

I used to smoke cigarettes rolled by hand, and every time I got in the car to go to work, I would roll before setting off. It eventually became a habit to roll a cigarette when I got in the car, even if I had just finished one not too long ago. I used to roll it and keep it in the center of the dashboard. It was just a habit to roll as I got in the car. That was just what I did.

There is absolutely zero doubt among the habit experts of the world that location is the most significant factor when it comes to mindlessly engaging in thoughts and activity. I write this book after the (hopefully) worst part of the COVID-19 pandemic is over, and it's incredible to see how many people were affected by the work-from-home solution.

I spoke to many friends and family about this who traveled to an office to work but instead worked from home. Because their office was associated with work, they could focus and get on with their to-do list. This is because the moment they stepped into the building or even got in the car to go to work, their brain told them they were at work, and this was where things got done.

On the other hand, when they arrived home from work, their brain disconnected from the idea of work and connected with the idea of being at home. Many people found it hard to integrate a work-from-home lifestyle because these lines were blurred so quickly. Home suddenly became a place of work *and* relaxation, which made it incredibly hard to focus because of all the locational cues. Places in the home that were meant for resting were now places of work, which sent a ton of conflicting signals to the brain.

Easy Self-Discipline

This is why I work at home with a home office. For many years, especially while I was living with my parents, I would work with a desk in my bedroom, and it was awful. I was incredibly unproductive because it was a room associated with sleep and rest. Likewise, I had so much trouble sleeping because when my brain was trying to rest, it was also thinking about work.

Interestingly, as I write this, I have a friend visiting Oregon this weekend, and the only time I've been to Oregon was to see my ex-girlfriend, who lived there for a bit. As I started receiving pictures of the scenery they were exploring, I couldn't help but feel sad because my only connection to that place was inevitably a bad breakup.

And even as I write this, I'm thinking about that breakup. I can feel myself replaying certain scenes of it, and immediately, I feel the craving to go downstairs and get myself a piece of Swiss chocolate roll I know is in the fridge. This is a cue literally based on a location that I'm receiving pictures of, even just the idea of a place since I haven't actually been to the location shown in the photographs.

Cue	Craving	Response	Reward

| I'm writing about a past breakup and feel sad about it. | I want to feel better. | I eat a piece of chocolate cake. | I'll get a dopamine hit from eating chocolate cake. |

Can you see how simple it is to have a trail of events leading from one habitual response to another? If you're really able to pay attention to yourself, you'll start to notice when you have certain feelings come up and the craving that comes as a result of it. This is mostly how you spend your life.

You wake and trigger a whole load of habits you call your routine. As specific times of the day come and you move from place to place, other cues trigger you, and other habits kick in. You go on Facebook because it's the first thing you do as you sit down on your lunch break and you see a photo of your ex. This triggers feelings and emotions and, depending on how you've dealt with those feelings and emotions in the past, you'll get a craving to sort it out.

Think about this in your own life and how certain locations will have certain habits and actions associated with them. Write them down using the same table formulae as this:

Cue	Craving	Response	Reward
You get to work.	You want to stop feeling sluggish and tired.	You make a cup of coffee before heading to your desk.	You feel awake.
You see a photo of your ex on Facebook.	You want to stop feeling sad about it.	You eat some cake.	You feel a little better.

As a recap, here are some of the cues you might want to focus on:

- The time of day
- The locations you're in
- Your emotional state
- External triggers like who you're with, people you see

- Content you see
- An event happening
- People you're around

Taking Control of Your Habit Cues

This is the first action in this book where you can start seeing change instantly. If you can follow through with the steps laid out in this section, some of which we've already spoken about, it's possible to experience instant change.

Because you're trying to reduce the likelihood of your bad habits taking place, this is what we're going to focus on first. There are four ways you can make a habit less appealing and reduce the effect that the cue is going to take place.

- You make the cue as nonexistent as possible
- You make the habit unappealing
- You make the habit difficult
- You make the habit unrewarding

This technique is based on the ideas that James Clear talks about in his *Atomic Habits* bestseller, and there's no denying such tactics have changed the lives of hundreds of thousands of people around the world. However, it doesn't matter which high performer or "successful" person you look at or feel inspired by, they will follow through with a similar technique based on the same strategies.

Your body and your being will always have needs. That's obvious. You will always feel some kind of reward of varying intensity when you fulfill that need. If you're addicted to Vegas slot machines, you'll get a hit of dopamine every time you pull that lever, whether you win nothing or hit the jackpot. It's the intensity of that reward that varies.

To go further, studies have shown that it's actually the anticipation of the reward that gets the dopamine going. In the slot machine example, pulling the lever and watching the reels spin and the sounds play sends the brain into overdrive because it's thinking, "Oh my god. This is it. This is where we win big!" This is why it can be addictive to play since your brain is already sending dopamine into your brain as the reward is coming.

Interestingly, this is not only fulfilling the need of being entertained but winning a jackpot will fulfill your financial needs and provide security in your life, which is why the possibility of winning big can be so intense. You're anticipating fulfilling your needs on a massive scale.

This is why your mouth can water at the very idea of food, not just while you're eating it. Remember we spoke about that at the beginning?

In the context of this book, the cue sets up this anticipation and makes the craving even more appealing because you want that reward so badly. This is why we want to focus on adjusting or removing the cues altogether.

The only real aspect of the loop you have control over is the cue that triggers the craving in the first place or the response you use, but it's always going to be easier to have control over that cue. If you don't experience the cue, you won't have the craving, won't follow through with the response, and so on. It's harder to change any other aspect because it's already set in stone within your neural pathways.

Let's break this down properly.

Mastering the Cue's Existence

If you're spending too much time on your phone, you'll be subject to several cues.

This could be the notifications pinging, the sight of your phone next to you, or a pang of loneliness or the fear of missing out (FOMO). All are valid cues. In this case, you can make the cue as nonexistent as possible by putting your phone in another room, leaving it at home while you go out, putting it on silent, or turning it off altogether.

We spoke about tactics like this earlier in the chapter. To break it down, you need to:

- Identify the cues of your bad habits
- Reduce the appearance of that cue in your life as much as possible

Now on the flip side, there has to be a positive habit in your life to fulfill the need the bad habit was fulfilling. Remember, the need in your brain is never going to go away just like that. Let's say you're trying to lose weight.

Using this tactic, you're going to stop buying junk food so there's no junk food in your fridge that you can just help yourself to at a moment's notice. Even if you're in a shared living situation where other people are eating junk food, even hiding the junk food behind food in the fridge or deeper into cupboards can be enough to stop you from eating it or seeing it when you open the cupboard and are triggered.

Think about desks in offices that have a plate of donuts on the table in the meeting, or people who keep bags of candy in the dashboard of their car or top drawer of their desk. Because these cues to eat are right in plain sight, the chances are that if the plate or bags of candy was out of view, say the sweets were in the glove box, the cue is removed, and the chances of you eating one are massively reduced.

On the other hand, you can use this tactic to improve the chances of you introducing a new habit into your life by simply doing the opposite.

Let's say you want to learn how to play the guitar or read more books. By placing more books around your house, such as leaving one on your bedside table or pillow or putting your guitar in plain sight at a key point in your home, instead of letting it gather dust in the cupboard, you're sending the cue to your brain that this is something you need to be thinking about.

Mastering the Cue's Appeal

Not all cues can be reduced. You're not going to hide your TV every time you're done watching, or if you're trying to quit smoking, the chances are you're going to see and smell other people smoking as you go about your day-to-day life. Some cues are simply unavoidable.

If this is the case, let's say you're quitting smoking and you're surrounded by people at work who also smoke. You need to make the habit look unappealing. You can do this by looking into the adverse health effects of smoking or adding up all the money you'd averagely spend on cigarettes and seeing the total. Since smokers tend to spend a lot of money on the habit, you could imagine all the other things you could spend it on.

It's tricks like this that make the bad habit unappealing. Of course, this requires a degree of imagination, but it's certainly a tactic that works when combined with the other strategies detailed in this chapter.

For me personally, I found that talking about the habit out loud to myself before I did it was a great way to stop me in my tracks. I basically got into the habit of saying what I was doing out loud in this way throughout my whole life. It was really simple to implement and a compelling way of making my existing habits less attractive.

I learned this technique from a friend who was suffering from a porn/sex addiction and was attending rehab sessions to deal with it, where he learned it from another person who had used the service to help themselves and now volunteered there.

Say you were on Instagram and you saw a picture of a model or your ex or whoever, and your mind started thinking about sexual fantasies. You get the craving to fulfill that sexual need, and you know it's going to lead to watching porn. It's in moments like this that you say to yourself, "I'm going to go to bed and watch porn and masturbate, but I know it's going to make me feel shame and guilt afterward because it's not something I want to do."

You're taking the mindless, habitual thought process and addressing it differently by saying it out loud. You're cutting off the trail of thought from routine thinking to mindful thinking, and suddenly the act doesn't seem too appealing. This is because it's easy to mentally dismiss the consequential feelings of shame and guilt because your brain is craving the dopamine from the response of masturbating.

Same with junk food. By going to the fridge and seeing the cue of a cake you don't really want to eat, you can say, "I am going to eat this cake, even though I know it's something I don't want to eat because I am looking after myself."

This might feel like you're trying to trick yourself, but remember, you don't really want to masturbate, smoke, or binge eat. You want a solution to a problem or a fix for a feeling you have.

This is where the other side of this point ties in. You can't just say you're not going to do something because you're saying it out loud. You still need to fulfill the need you're addressing. Let's say you're feeling stressed and crave smoking. You could say something like, "I'm going to meditate/go for a walk/write a journal entry because I'm feeling stressed, and I know this is good for me in the long term."

You don't even need to mention smoking. You're fulfilling the need in an alternative, more beneficial way. It's essential you include saying why you're using the alternative habit because this will make it attractive.

Yes, it can feel bizarre saying this kind of thing out loud. Try saying one of the sentences above, and it can feel a little awkward and embarrassing, but it's such a powerful technique. Just give it a try for a week, and you'll see the difference. The real trick to mastering this approach is by saying what you're doing out loud, even when it's seemingly nothing. Become your own proof.

For example, you could say, "I'm drinking water now because I know it's going to make me healthier and happier," or "I'm brushing my teeth because I don't want to lose my teeth, get a toothache, or suffer from bad breath."

Mastering the Cue's Difficulty

This is similar to removing the cue altogether, but if you're dealing with a habit you can't avoid, then making the habit as difficult as possible is a great way to stop yourself from doing it. Remember, habits are designed by nature to make your life as easy as possible. This is why it's seemingly effortless to indulge in "bad" behavior. Your brain is wired to do it without thinking, and you unconsciously create your life in a way that makes it even easier (leaving cues out, putting snacks in your top drawer, and so on).

This part of the strategy plays on this because if the bad habit is far more complex and requires a lot more effort than the good habit you're trying to introduce, then you're naturally going to want to go through with the good habit because it means you have to exert less energy. Go back to the example we had on having donuts on the table and imagine if they were now on the other side of the room.

Imagine your kitchen table, and you had a stack of chocolate bars or candies you could help yourself to at any time. The chances are you'd go through your kitchen and help yourself to one whenever you had the chance. That's not good for your health, even if it feels good in the short term.

Alternatively, let's say you move the chocolate bars into the very back end of a cupboard in the corner of your kitchen that you rarely go near and instead put a bowl of fruit in the center of the table. Every time you go through your kitchen, your brain is hardwired to take something off the table (the table or even entering the kitchen could be a cue), and it's far easier to grab a piece of fruit than it is a bar of chocolate; thus, you start forming the positive habit of eating healthy.

Mastering the Cue's Satisfaction

As we discussed earlier, you got through the response part of the habit loop, and your brain feels good because it fulfilled a need. It's satisfying to do so, so the final part of this process is to make the bad habits unsatisfying and the good habits as satisfying as possible.

This is typically extremely hard work because we live in a world where instant gratification is forced down our throats. Amazon delivers the next day, and likes and comments are pinged to our phones in an instant. This means that working on long-term goals like getting fit or writing a book can get easily sidelined because you're instead chasing the endless pursuit of short term, fast hits of satisfaction.

So how do you make a night in front of the TV less appealing than spending a few hours in the gym? Sounds impossible, right?

Well, using the techniques above, you've already started to take a step towards making the satisfaction of your bad habits lower. By saying, "I'm not going to watch porn because I'm not a sex addict that everyone will know me to be," whether or not it's true, you're creating a frame of mind where your brain says, "Hey, I don't want people to know me as a sex addict." Suddenly reputation becomes more important than the desire to masturbate.

This can also be helped massively when you have an accountability partner or someone you work alongside on your habit journey, but we'll talk about that more later.

On the other hand, making your good habits more satisfying is actually relatively easy when you start thinking creatively. The trick is not to think about the long-term gains and how you're missing out now, but rather how you can bring short-term satisfaction to these ventures.

For example, as a marketer and writer, I spend the majority of my day writing, but even this book I'm writing now is only ever going to have feedback or some kind of payoff in months, possibly even years to come. The satisfaction is a long way off, which doesn't help me sit down and write every day, so I need to find a way to make the process of writing for hours every single day interesting and rewarding now.

Based on a story in *Atomic Habits,* I purchased two small wooden bowls that you would usually serve chip dip in and a small bag of marbles.

They're set up in front of me as I write this, and one bowl is empty, and the other is full of marbles. Using a little word counting app that shows me how many words I've written, I move one marble into the empty bowl every time I finish writing or editing a thousand words. As the day goes on, the smaller bowl starts to fill with marbles, and it's incredibly satisfying because it's a solid and consistent visual representation that I'm doing well. The simple act of moving a marble across shows that I'm making actual, tangible progress.

What's more, to my right, I have an open diary with each A5 page broken into two halves that cover two days. I have bullet-pointed my to-do list for the day and each corner as three metrics that I'm working on. I have how much money I've earned from client work, I have a section for how many words I've written in total, and I have how many hours of sleep I got that night.

Each and every day, the moment I finish an item on my to-do list, I cross it off. The trick here is to cross off as the first thing you do when you finish the task, way before you even think about moving on to the next thing. You need that action of crossing off, so your brain says, "Yes, I achieved something," and gets the dopamine hit. This is how you take control of your human nature and use it to your advantage.

The moment I've written 1,000 words, I move a marble across to get that dopamine hit and to keep the momentum flowing. At the end of the day, I total up my metric counts, and I do something as simple as a smiley face next to each metric when I've hit my target. If I've had a good day, I allow myself an hour or two of video games or TV before bed. I'll go and see a friend or have a day out somewhere weekly as a reward for having a good week.

Don't try to work against human nature, nor should you try to ignore it or overcome it. Integrate tactics into your life that take advantage of how your brain is wired and let it help you become the person you want to be. Work with the grain of your brain!

Over to You

And that's it. Now you know how to drop your bad habits and create good ones. Good luck and all the best. I'm only joking; we have a bit more to cover just yet, but that is essentially the basics you need to know when it comes to forming good habits in your life and ultimately becoming the person you want to be.

Simply to summarize the chapter, you need to:

- Take your habits and identify the cues
- Work on reducing the cues of the negative habits in your life
- Create new cues for the habits you do want to create
- Make things as simple as possible

- Make your bad habits nonexistent, unappealing, difficult, or unsatisfying to do

Chapter Five - Creating the Perfect Environment for Success

"We first make our habits, and then our habits make us." - John Dryden

We've spoken a bit about how your environment is essential when it comes to successfully mastering your habits and nudging yourself towards becoming the best version of yourself—location being one of the most important cues there is.

You know that your environment is filled with cues that trigger the habit loops you have in your life, and that mastery of your environment and, therefore, these cues is essential to your habit-changing success.

While we've covered some basic tips already, I'd like to dedicate this chapter to the art of environmental design because it has such a massive impact on whether you succeed or not. Think about a drug addict. I've known a few in my life. These were high school friends who ended up in rehab for their addictions that stemmed from various reasons. They got clean, yet once they found themselves back in the real world, they relapsed, and the whole process began again. Statistics show that around 80 percent of addicts will relapse in their first year.

The main problem here is entirely on the environment that the individual is in.

Let's say you're a teen drug addict. Not a hardcore user, but you used to love getting high and partying with your friends, but recently your usage has become a little more frequent. You're using when you're on your own at home, and you feel stressed when you can't get a hit. You realize you have a mild problem and would like to cut back. Yet while you can work on cutting back and managing your cravings, as soon as you're around your friends again, you can't seem to help but use again, and then you start using at home again, and you're back at square one.

Think of the environments you'd be a part of. Whether you're at parties, a friend's house, or in your local park, these are all environments that your brain associated with drug use. Both the people you're around and the places you're in are the cues that trigger the habit loop. Your problem becomes more serious over time because the more you follow through with these habit loops, the more ingrained in your brain they become.

Eventually, you have an intervention, and you're sent off to rehab. Miraculously, you get clean rather quickly, and you don't even crave the drugs. Why? Because you're in a new environment. In rehab, there are no drugs. There are no cues, and you're in a place that is actively promoting a life without drugs. You find it easy because the cues are literally nonexistent, and you have a cue to fulfill whatever need you were taking drugs for, whether that was counseling or group activities.

Now you're clean, you head back to your hometown, and low and behold, you're back to your old habits. To cut a long story short, you're back in the same environment with your old triggers and cues, so it's effortless for your brain to fall back into those habits. It isn't until new systems and habits are in place that this looping effect can begin to change, which leads us back to environmental design.

You are far more reliant on environmental cues than you think. Research backs this up.

One study proved this by looking into students and their habits while at university. Stereotypically speaking, students are renowned for their somewhat bad habits. They discovered that students who transferred to another university were the most likely to adopt new daily routines because they weren't exposed to familiar environmental cues and triggers of their existing habit loops, which could be found all over their old university campus. These were cues developed from their existing time in their original university. Once transferred, they easily picked up new habits compared to the control group of habit changers who stayed in their original posting because the cues were fresh and were yet to develop.

There's plenty of research out there on this kind of stimulus control theory, or really simply put, cause and effect. All your behaviors are affected by external triggers. I've spoken already about how such triggers can affect what we eat, when we eat, and how we sleep.

You've perhaps heard of other common analogies here that run along the same principles.

You'll eat more if you use a large spoon or serve your meal up on a large dish. You'll lose weight and consume fewer calories if you move the small bowl of chocolates on your desk six feet away. You'll forget how much you ate if you eat chicken wings without the bones on the table, thus eating more.

Your outside world is very much in control of your inside world if you let it be that way. However, now that we've opened this door, you can start to take control of your external triggers and use them to your advantage. By this, I mean you can change your cues to reduce the likelihood of engaging in a bad habit and develop new environmental cues to help you master new ones that you consciously want to bring into your life.

Change Your Environment. Change Your Life

Discipline cannot be relied on. While it's essential at some points in your life, like a muscle, it can wear thin pretty quickly and will leave you when it matters most. Discipline and willpower are great if you need a short burst of strictness to deal with something, but it can't be used every hour of every day, which is why we need an approach like the ones detailed in this book.

So, let's introduce another one based on environmental design strategies.

The Power of Associating

You associate tasks with places, people, rooms, and other tasks all the time. You associate the gym with working out, your office with working, your bed with sleep, and so on. Take control of this and divide up the spaces in your life.

For example, the bedroom should only be used for sleeping. That means no phones, no television, perhaps a book at a push. Nothing stimulating, apart from the obvious (wink wink), should be associated with the bedroom because it's where you want to sleep with ease, and you know how important sleep is to your health and well-being.

On the other hand, your lounge should only be used for leisure activities, such as reading, playing games, playing on your phone, and so on. It can take a little while for these new habits to form as you're creating new associations, but this is where you'll have a powerful advantage and your system set up to help you if you have an accountability buddy.

Remember at the beginning of the book about how I said this journey of habit growth should be looked at as an adventure? Instead of mindlessly going through life lost in your own endless cycling habits, you can take control, aim big, and see where you end up because of it. This is a great mindset to have when approaching strategies like this.

Basically, set up cues to keep these spaces their own spaces. Keep your phone on the counter in the lounge, so you associate the relaxing area of your house with phone time. Keep a book on your pillow so you're setting up the cue to read before you go to sleep. Remember, it's not so much about actually reading. Even just opening the book and reading a sentence is 1 percent better than yesterday, and these results will compound over time.

Encourage you and your partner to follow the same rules and set up these boundaries. Do so with excitement because you'll start seeing the benefits almost immediately; benefits that will start to build and build the more you do them, which will only motivate you to keep going.

You'll sleep better, eat better, have better control over your technology usage, and far better time management skills. Ultimately, this will make you happier, less depressed, less anxious, and genuinely have a lot more energy to go about your day.

Even if you don't have much space at home, you have an entire world to explore. This is the reason why writers are renowned for going to sit in coffee shops. If you visit a specific cafe a few times and only work there, you'll notice how much more focused you get even walking in the store because your brain associates the place with work and work alone.

Managing Task Friction

When I talk about friction, I'm talking about the amount of resistance there between a thought occurring (a cue) and taking action. If you're sitting at the desk and the donuts are in front of you, you'll happily keep picking at them and scarfing them down simply because they are there in front of you. There's no friction in the action of sitting and taking a donut.

However, even the simple act of having them on the other side of the desk, just out of reach, is enough to put you off and lower your consumption instantly. Humans really are somewhat basic when it comes to behavioral actions like this, and it's fascinating.

So instead of just letting the world control you in such a way that you're acting mindlessly, it's time to take control of yourself and your own thought patterns by making jobs and actions in your life either harder or easier. In short, add or reduce friction for the habits in your life as you see fit.

If you're spending too much time on your phone, add a lock screen, or there are apps that lock your phone for a set amount of time. This creates friction to unlock it, making you less likely to use it. This is why website blockers can be so effective when used correctly.

This is why so many habit experts and gurus will talk about the power of goals or actual lack of them. Goals are great because they push you in the direction you want to go and help you know what to focus on. Your goal could be to become fit and healthy, or it could be to write a book. However, setting these goals is only a worthwhile pastime if they help inspire the actions and behaviors you need to get there (i.e., going to the gym or sitting down and writing pages).

This is where the difference lies. You don't want to spend all your energy on trying to get strong at the gym or sitting down and writing a novel out of thin air. Instead, spend a large portion of your energy on making the task as simple as possible.

From an environmental standpoint, this makes the difference between choosing a gym that's located along the same route you drive home from work on, as opposed to signing up for a gym that's located on the other side of town.

It's the difference between keeping your guitar, your running shoes, your bike, and your healthy food blender in the back of the cupboards or garages and placing them front and center within your home. It's the difference between keeping your phone in your pocket or next to you at your desk or burying it deep into the bottom drawer of your bedside table while you go out for the day.

Add the things you want to do into your life, and remove the distractions you don't want. There are going to be times where you think to yourself, *Ah, whatever,* and you'll just want to go and indulge yourself in whatever bad habit you're trying to break, but the harder you make this to do, the more likely you'll be to overcome the craving.

Again, you're going to slip up and relapse. Science shows it's pretty much guaranteed unless you physically overhaul your life and move to a different country where nothing is the same, but even if you're getting 1 percent better every day, that's far better than zero. In essence, I'm saying use your laziness to your advantage. We're human beings. We all do it.

Put Good Things in Good Places

Hand in hand with the consideration above, if there's something you want to do with your life, set it up so it's impossible to fail. For example, starting a running habit can be created by simply developing the habit of putting your running shoes on and walking up the road. To enhance this further, place your running shoes in a place where you're always going to see them, thus setting up the cue that you want to go running.

Now, this can backfire if you're not careful, especially if you get into the habit of ignoring your shoes when you see them, and then that becomes the habit, and it's going to make you feel terrible. Instead, break the task down and make it easy. Put your shoes on and step outside. Even if you step back in and take them off again, make this your new habit. When it's a habit, then step things up and run to the end of your street and back.

This can feel so stupid, especially if you're using this example literally, but I can't stress enough how much more beneficial it is to do something like this than run once every six months while hoping it sticks one day, which it's never going to do with that approach.

As you can see, the importance of mastering your environment is perhaps your most important key to success, and it should never be underestimated. Instead, it should be a priority in your life.

Chapter Six - Making Your New Habits Effortless

"As you simplify your life, the laws of the universe will be simpler; solitude will not be solitude, poverty will not be poverty, nor weakness weakness." – Henry David Thoreau

At this stage, you could go out into the world and start bringing all those habits you wish you could do into your life. It's very possible. You have the tools and everything you need, but you need to overcome a few more obstacles.

Let's face it, the idea of mindlessly being able to go for a run would be amazing. Imagine waking up, and without even having to think about it, you just popped your running shoes on, and away you went. That would be the dream, but life doesn't work that way. It requires effort to do such tasks, and this is where you may feel like you're being held back. You might say to yourself that you simply don't have the energy to get up and go for a run, and that's why you sit in front of the TV. You just don't have it in you.

It's all well and good mastering your cues and making them appealing and so on, but if you don't have the supposed willpower to get up and do the good thing, you're never going to be able to do it. Right? Well, firstly, willpower is a myth, and we've already covered that, so you can consider that a smack on the wrist if you thought that was the case. But, I see where you're coming from, which is why we're now going into this section of the book, which is all about making your habits effortless. Even in the case of intense, more challenging activities, like going for a run, it is very possible.

You Only Need to Master Showing Up

Going back to what we were saying about short- and long-term gain, going for a run is a prime example. If you go for a run and you're not already the most athletic person, then chances are you're going to be terrible at it. You won't run far, nor will you be fast at it, and it's probably going to feel quite embarrassing. If you're at the gym and everyone else is seemingly better than you, this can be very off-putting.

What's more, you're not going to get better after a single run. You'll get a small hit of dopamine for exercising, but it's clear the cons are certainly outweighing the pros. The chances are you'd try it and then give up, falling back into your old habitual ways of doing things.

Unfortunately, we've spoken about this already, so you're about to get another slap on the wrist! If you're living life in this way and you're trying to form new habits, you need to stop thinking about the response and the reward but instead focus on the journey. Yes, you know the long-term benefits of running, but using what we spoke about in the last chapter, you need to make it satisfying now.

This is where the art of showing up comes into play, and this was probably the most beneficial aspect of habit mastery that I learned on my own journey and am still learning today, so I'm very excited to share it with you.

When it comes to introducing habits in your life, the real trick to mastering them and turning otherwise complex tasks into effortless actions is simple. You scale down the habit until you find yourself at the most basic step, and then you aim to get the habit of only doing that step. When you step yourself up so you can't possibly fail, you're allowing yourself to excel.

Let's say you want to be a writer. Writing a book (which is the long-term result) is a long and complicated process. It's a journey where publishing your book is the end goal, but in itself, it's a goal that's too vague and actionless to make any progress and thus develop the habit of writing that will eventually turn into a published book. Instead, let's break it down.

What does writing and publishing a book entail?

- Research

- Outlining
- Writing
- Drafting
- Editing
- Designing a cover
- Marketing
- Applying to agents

No, you see, these are still steps that are far too vague. Granted, they're more specific, but you're still setting yourself up for a loss because these are big goals. If you start researching but you find you're not getting anywhere, then you'll feel like you'll have wasted your time. If you feel like this, you'll start looking for short-term satisfaction to fill the void, and you'll fall back into your old habits of not writing.

With this in mind, we're going to set one simple habit: I will sit down at my computer every single day.

Do you think this is a habit you could manage? That's it. That's all you have to do. I'm sure you're able to complete an action like this. By doing this simple act alone and saying yes, I've done this habit (because it's so simple to achieve). However, while a simple habit is already achieved, you're opening the doorway to then sit down and write your book.

This is because when you sit down at your computer, you can tick this off your list, and since you're already sat down, you may as well start working on your book.

You can apply this to any new, positive habit you want to introduce to your life. If you want to start running, make the habit the simple act of putting your shoes on. If you want to learn how to cook, make your habit one where you turn on the oven. If you want to learn the guitar, make your habit of plucking each string just once.

Such simple actions are practically effortless but have such a big effect because you're:

- Ticking a box and receiving a reward for doing something you set out to do
- Putting yourself in a position where you can start working on the larger aspect of your habit

Once you've taken this action, you then want to keep your simple habits flowing. If you're writing a book, set a habit of writing just 50 words or researching just one point. If you're running and you've just tied your shoes, make your next habit of stepping out the door and walking out to the road. If you're learning the guitar, make your next habit of opening your lesson book or opening up an online tutorial.

Again, you're keeping the habit so small and so effortless that you can't miss it. You're making it basically impossible to fail.

Now, this is the important bit. It doesn't matter if you stop there. Ninety percent of the time, getting a little rush of dopamine is enough to keep the momentum going and keep you moving forward with your task (more on this in a bit), but the trick is to master the art of showing up. That's all. Remember what we talked about in the introduction where you can get 1 percent better every day, and you'd be 37 times better in just one year? This is what I was talking about.

Even if you're putting on your running shoes and then taking them off again, as long as you can make it a habit to show up and do that each and every day, you're better off than you were. When you're doing this simple action effortlessly and have formed the habit, then you take it up to the next level. In this case, you could run to the end of the road and back and so on.

This may seem stupid or pointless. Why would you put running shoes on and take them off again? Simple: you're building the habit. It's either this approach or continuously getting motivated one day, going for a run, hating yourself because you suck, and then not doing it again until you're feeling motivated again, which brings us to a very important point.

How to Do Things Even When It's Hard

The whole idea behind this approach of mastering the art of showing up, rather than trying to master whatever the end result of your life is, is to make your life easy and your ventures effortless. However, the difference between the people who make it in life and the people who don't are those who show up each and every day, even when they don't feel like it.

You talk to any top athlete, and they'll tell you the same thing. The best in the world aren't necessarily the people who have the best technique, are the fastest, or the strongest. They're the people who train and exercise and monitor their nutrition day in, day out. Even when nobody's looking. Sure, competing in an event or at the Olympics looks exciting and intense, but nobody sees the hours upon hours in the gym doing the same reps day after day.

It's going to be boring. It's going to get tedious. There will be endless points throughout your journey where the satisfaction of doing a repetitive task, no matter how much you break down and try to make it rewarding, will wear thin, and you'll be bored. You'll want to give up. There are going to be times where you do give up.

So when these days inevitably come around, what can you do to pick yourself up and carry on?

Firstly, you need to make sure you're getting straight back onto the path you just left if you relapse. If you fall out of routine for one day, the best thing you can do is to pick yourself up and carry on from where you left off as soon as possible. If you've set yourself up with the habit of getting up at six in the morning, but you had a late night, something came up, and now you're up at seven or eight, you're probably feeling pretty bad about it. You had managed to stay on track, and now you're slipping.

It's going to feel like you're heading back the way you came, but it's important to remember that you're not. There is no human being on the planet that is perfect, regardless of what your partner might have you believe, and you're bound to make mistakes. You just need to accept this and just pick yourself up.

There's no point in beating yourself up because you made a mistake or letting things slip further because what's the point, what's done is done, and so on. Just notice that something has happened, accept it, and get back on the horse in the direction you plan to go.

Then, if you're struggling to get going, once again, make it, so you're mastering the art of turning up, and that's it. If you're at home and you're supposed to go to the gym, and you're not really feeling like it, go to the gym and go for a swim instead, or just sit in the sauna. Even if you go to the gym, get changed, sit on a mat for five minutes, and then go home, it's this simple act of showing up that will make you progress in the long run. I literally know people who have done just this and will go to the gym, sit in the car park for five minutes, and then go home.

It doesn't seem like much and may feel like a waste of time, but it's actions like this that help you become 1 percent better every day. Make your habits as easy as possible so you can't fail. The longer you can stick with them and the more consistently you can show up, the easier it will get over time.

How to Involve Other People for Greater Success

You've probably heard of the term "accountability partner," but just so we're on the same page, let's explore what that means. If you haven't, then welcome to your introduction! An accountability partner is basically someone in your life that you involve in your habit-building process, and typically you'll get involved in theirs. The aim of this is to hold each other accountable for your actions and your behaviors. In 12-step rehab programs, this is a core aspect of the program as you will be paired with a mentor (someone who has gone through the rehab journey), and once you're clean, you'll become a mentor to someone else.

Instead of struggling and facing the difficulties and celebrating the wins of your journey alone, you'll have someone there alongside you. As Christopher McCandless shares in the movie and book based on a real story, happiness is only real when shared.

When it comes to habit-building, having an accountability partner is one of the best techniques there is.

You check in with your partner each day to tell them how you're getting on. This method works on basic human principles because you don't want to look bad in front of the other person, thus being held accountable for what you do. Let's say you're trying to eat healthily, and you're cutting down on junk food.

If you cave and give in to a craving and you're going through the process alone, it's easy to dismiss the hiccup and push down those feelings of guilt, at least in the short term. On the other hand, if someone in your life knows all about it, you don't want to let them down or look bad in their eyes, making it less likely you'll cave.

While it's essential to hold yourself accountable at all times, it's equally essential to be accountable to others and have others hold you accountable. Of course, this means that you need to pick the right person to be your accountability partner, which is what we're going to explore now.

Perhaps surprisingly, there's no right or wrong way to choose an accountability partner that will work for you, so you must trust your abilities to choose supportive people you know you can trust. This can be tricky. For example, if your family is a little dysfunctional or you have friends who don't really understand what you're doing or what habit change is, you may subconsciously choose someone who will cause you more harm than good.

However, you first need to discover what kind of habits you want to change and what approach you want to take. There will be people in your life who can be kind and supportive as accountability partners, but there will be others who will be stern, strict, and will aim to push you.

You might not be pushed hard enough for the transformation to work if your accountability partner is too validating. It can also backfire if your accountability partner is excessively strict and demanding, and you may not feel understood, leading you to give up altogether. You may benefit from either. It's entirely up to you and your own way of learning and growing.

Don't forget, it's always going to be better if you're working with someone who is also working on their habits, so you can keep them accountable as well. This way, you'll have a give and take relationship where you're helping each other, rather than it being one-sided. Choosing an accountability partner in this way comes down to what works best for you and your partner. Nevertheless, whatever approach you pick or what type of person you want, you should pick someone who is nonjudgmental and someone you feel comfortable sharing your true feelings with.

If you find yourself hiding the truth from your accountability partner, then you need to ask yourself whether you need to work on being more open or if you've chosen the right person to work with at all. If you're hiding the facts or even lying about sticking to your habits when you're not, there's clearly a problem that needs to be addressed.

Don't worry, you're not the only one who does this. Many people lie to their physical trainers or life coaches. It's statistically proven that around 25 percent of patients will also lie to their doctor about their health habits and life decisions, perhaps out of shame or guilt for whatever the habit is.

To break it down a little further, there are three main types of accountability partners you'll choose to work with.

Those Who Are Ahead of You

To feel inspired to want to change, you will pick a partner who is "ahead of you," or basically where you want to be. You'll be following in their footsteps and basically viewing this person as a mentor who will be able to guide you to where they are.

A Motivating Individual

A motivating individual is someone who will have your best interests at heart. They aim to inspire and motivate you to make the right decisions, help you explore your options, and encourages you to do the best you can. They will also provide support when the going gets tough and you start to lean off your path.

Someone on the Same Level

Many benefits can come from having an accountability partner who is in the same place you are, the most prevalent of which is the fact that you'll encounter similar problems simultaneously, thus being able to address them and overcome them together. If you feel slightly alone in your habit change pursuits, getting this kind of partner can change everything.

So, how do you find the person that's best suited to you and your ventures? Here are some criteria to remember. You're looking for:

- A person who does not pass judgment.
- Someone who recognizes that relapse is a natural part of the recovery process and views these periods as learning opportunities rather than embarrassments.
- Someone with whom you are at ease.

Don't forget you need to be the same as the other person. You need to be the person you want your accountability partner to be to you.

It can take some time to find the right person, the person you feel comfortable with, so don't feel like you're forced to rush into this. You may have flippant conversations with your friends, but if it doesn't feel right and you don't feel motivated, don't feel pressured to commit. List your prospects and get some ideas.

Once you start having an idea of someone you want to work with, begin by having a full, open, and honest conversation and start thinking of a time you'll always get in touch. Consistency is key to a successful relationship, and make sure you're precise.

Are you going to chat in the early morning, on your lunch breaks, evenings, or weekends? How frequently are you going to talk? Will you get in touch once a day, once a week, or twice a week? How will you keep in touch, whether it's by text, email, FaceTime, phone call, coffee date, or meeting up and going for a walk? The more specific you can be, the more likely you are to stick with your commitments.

Finally, here are some other considerations you'll want to think about when it comes to working with an accountability partner.

Set Boundaries and Ground Rules

Talk about when you're communicating and how you will. You need to express what kind of expectations you have and what you want the other person to offer. Make sure you take the time to understand what the other person needs from you and how you can help them. You need to have this conversation at the start before you start moving forward.

Give Frequent Feedback

I'm not just talking about giving feedback on the other person and how they achieved their goals, but also on their support style. Are they fulfilling your needs? Are they meeting your expectations? As a rule of thumb, give feedback more often than you receive it.

If you agree to check in every day, check in every day. Make your partnership a high priority in your life. The more effort you put in, the more effort they put in, and so the momentum builds. What's more, helping others not only boosts your happiness and life satisfaction, it will help you stay focused on your own goals.

Be Gentle Yet Firm

When your accountability partner falls, trips up, makes a mistake, or relapses, it's not on you to approach them aggressively and to put them down. This is the opposite of what you want to do. You need to be thoughtful and compassionate (think about how you want to be treated in such a situation) and then aim to nudge them back onto the path they want to be on. However, the style of your approach will depend on your initial conversations, as we spoke about above.

Develop Your Communication Skills

An effective and successful accountability relationship relies on one core principle: Effective Communication. If you've never done anything like this before, then the chances are you're not going to be very good at communication, or at the very least be in a place where you can certainly get better.

This means taking the time to practice your communications skills, whether you're reading communication books, practicing in front of the mirror, or watching tutorial videos. This is also a skill that will benefit you in all areas of your life.

Consistency is Everything

I really don't need to say more here. Master the art of showing up.

Accept Responsibility for Mistakes and Errors

Both you and your partner are going to make mistakes and slip up, both in your own journeys and helping each other, and you must be able to see and own up to what you've done wrong and be proactive in making it better.

Remember, this is what this journey is all about. Becoming the best version of yourself, which means working on becoming the best version of yourself. If you fail to keep a promise (and we know that life can get in the way sometimes), own the mistake and be better next time.

Keep Your Appointments

That goes hand in hand with what I said above. Even if you're having a chat and you're not reaching the goals you set out to achieve, that's not really the point. Getting 1 percent better than you were yesterday is infinitely better than zero. It's about being consistent and showing up.

And with that, we come to the end of this chapter. Now, I'm aware that was a lot to take in, so if you want to pause and go away to think about everything you've just processed, I recommend you do so before coming back and moving on.

Chapter Seven - The Importance of Habit Tracking

"For a successful life, or successful business, measure what you want to improve." - Jerry Bruckner

When I started my own journey into mastering my habits, dropping my old ones, and developing my new ones, I started doing my research online and was instantly presented with the absolutely massive range of habit-tracking apps out there. You've probably seen them yourself. By far one of the most popular forms of apps on the market, there are apps with hundreds of thousands of downloads, and now all I see on my Instagram ads are adverts for these apps. There seems to be a new one coming out every week.

While I initially tried some of these apps, used up my free trials, and even paid for some subscriptions, I never found success with using them. In hindsight, this makes a lot of sense. I thought that downloading and installing an app would be all I needed to do to make my new habits stick and move forward in my life, but of course, that's not the case. These habit tracking apps, or any habit tracking system for that matter, are only an additional strategy to help improve the work you're doing.

Contrary to what many people believe when they sign up for a habit tracking app or start writing to-do lists, these activities won't help you improve your habits. It's just another tool to help you along the way. However—and this is a big however—when using these strategies in the right way, they can be incredibly powerful and beneficial to your efforts and can easily help you go a long way.

The Benefits of Habit Tracking

While there are many benefits to habit tracking, many of which will vary from person to person depending on how you use the strategy and what you plan to get out of using it in the first place, there are some general benefits it can bring into your life. Here are some of my personal favorites.

Consistent Progression Towards Goals

By far the most impactful benefit. As we've discussed, whether your end goal is to write a book or run a marathon, habits aren't this "end goal" you're trying to reach, but rather the small actions you make that will eventually get you there.

If you're able to make a habit of tracking your habits (which we'll explore below), this is yet another action that will help you create the behaviors you want to create and will ultimately help you get to where you're going on the journey you want to walk. Remember, small actions compound and create significant results over a long period of time. This is simply another behavior on this same line of thinking.

Reduce Negative Habits That Hold You Back

Before jumping into the rhyme and reason of why habit tracking can help you form new habits, it's equally important to talk about how habit tracking can be used in reverse (i.e., help you track habits you want to drop from your life).

For example, if you're watching porn every day, playing too many video games, smoking, or eating junk food, or basically doing something you know is not bringing any real value into your life, it's so easy to slip back into these ways of living your life if you're not proactively working on them and monitoring them. Habit tracking is another way to do just this.

Simply writing your behavior down as a "poor habit" will help you become more aware of it when you do it. By keeping track of your new habit's progress, you'll be able to hold yourself accountable for whether you engaged in the new replacement behavior or the bad one.

It's worth remembering that you're essentially leaving your progress up to chance if you're not tracking your progress. By writing down and monitoring your relapses, recording your streaks, and writing down your goals, you're bringing focus to the things in your life you want to have control over.

You Can Hold Yourself Accountable

Typically, you know which of your habits are good and bad, yet we often choose to perpetuate the poor behavior. We've spoken about this relapsing behavior, and it's very common throughout the initial stages of changing a habit because this is where you're trying to find a system that works for you. However, without the solid proof of action that habit tracking can provide, you lack the means to hold yourself accountable.

For example, you might be saying to yourself, "I'm working on it," when you're getting involved in a bad habit. I've spoken a little about my dependence on video games during my early twenties, and I would frequently find myself saying, "Oh, I'll just play one more game before bed, even though it's already 4 a.m."

Then, the little voice of reason would kick in and say, "Hey, are you really sure you want to do that? I think we should go to bed and get rested. This is the bad habit you keep thinking about."

To this, my brain that lacked systems and structures would say, "Hey, I'm thinking about it, and I'm aiming to get a better sleeping pattern. As long as I'm thinking about it, I'm working on it." I'm saying all these statements to myself to reassure myself that I'm actually making progress on my aims when in reality, I'm not.

Simply put, if you don't keep track of your progress, you may not realize you've been "working on it" for years. By writing down the habit and tracking, it allows you to see whether you're improving or not.

You Create the Opportunity for Momentum

There's no denying that habits can gain traction in a variety of ways.

As we've discussed, the first is that the more you practice a habit, the easier it becomes. The second reason is that after you've mastered one habit, you'll be eager to tackle another. You start to create momentum. Let's say you want to start working on creating a healthy lifestyle, and you want to do this by creating the perfect morning routine.

You want to wake up and meditate for ten minutes. Then you want to do some yoga or go for a run, write your to-do list out, and keep a mood journal, then you grab a coffee and start your day, whether that means going to work, doing some writing, or spending time with your family.

You break the process down and start meditating for ten minutes as soon as you get up. Once you've done this, and since you're using a habit tracking system, you tick the box that confirms that you're making progress. Because it feels incredibly positive to tick an item off your list and to see you're making progress quickly, you're inclined to move on to the next activity because you want to make more progress in this way.

This is the same process we spoke about when talking about the art of habit stacking, and using habit tracking is just another effective way to bring this strategy to life.

You Create Visual Progression

When you use a physical method to check off whatever habits you're getting done and successfully introduce or remove from your life, you're creating a visual representation of your progress, which works amazingly as motivation to keep going!

For example, if you see that you've woken up and actually got up every day on your first alarm for the previous 20 days, and you're unusually weary on day 21, you'll be less likely to hit the snooze button to avoid breaking your streak. Again, the power of habit stacking, but this time in a visual way that's far easier to progress.

When you're keeping your progress in your head, it's easy to forget what you've done or where you are, especially where you're wearily waking up at six in the morning. Track your progress for that extra boost of progression confirmation every time you look at it. Perhaps the most traditional way of doing this is to put an X on a calendar for every day you've achieved your desired goals.

What's more, keeping a visual record of your habit-tracking efforts in this way allows you to reflect on the challenges you've faced. Perhaps there is a recurring problem in your life that is causing you to slip up. Without a visual record, the chances are you're never going to identify this problem and overcome it.

When you can do this successfully, and you can again see the insane compounding progress you're making, you'll have far more confidence that will motivate you to take on bigger and bigger difficulties in the future.

A Huge Boost to Your Self-Confidence

Hand in hand with the consideration above, the more negative habits you break and the more positive habits you develop and start to see coming to fruition, the more confident you get in your ability to break more. Not only that, you'll start feeling so much more capable as a human being, which will make you more confident socially, more charismatic, and more friendly.

You know that shame and guilt you feel when you cave and relapse back into your old ways? It makes you depressed because it's a little reminder you're not in control and that your habits are running your life against your will. Of course you're going to feel bad, and it's going to affect all other areas of your life as a result.

On the other hand, when you see progress and that you are really in control thanks to all the systems you've successfully set up, the reverse happens, and your confidence and self-esteem begin to take off. You'll gain the confidence to take on more if you can give yourself tiny victories throughout the day.

A great example of this would be a morning routine where if you get up early, work out, eat a good breakfast, then listen to a motivational podcast on your way to work, you will feel energized and ready for the day. Even so early before you've even got to work, you already feel that you've accomplished so much, which gives you the confidence to take on even more challenges that come your way.

Compare this to someone who hits the snooze button ten times, rushes out of the house, and listens to dismal news on the drive to work. They won't have the same mindset or level of confidence, despite living in the same day.

Your Entire Life Starts to Improve

One of my favorite things about habits (and self-improvement in general) is that once you start improving one aspect of your life, it usually spreads to others.

For example, if you start being more strict about arriving to work on time, you'll probably start being more strict about arriving on time to other occasions as well! You may improve multiple areas at the same time by focusing on one!

Tips for Integrating Habit Tracking Strategies into Your Life

Now you're aware of the benefits of visually tracking your habits, we're going to jump into the meat of this chapter and see how you can successfully integrate habit tracking into your life. There are endless ways you can do this. Earlier, we spoke about how every 1,000 words I write, I move a marble across from one dish to another to create the opportunity to see my progress growing throughout the day.

This is a form of habit tracking. You could print off a calendar specifically for your habits or create a page in your journal, where you write down the habit and tick or cross the box for every day you're able to do it. You could download a habit tracking app for your smartphone or computer, or you could just keep a sheet of paper on your desk with all the habits you want to bring into your life and just tick a box every time you do it. It's really up to you, but I highly recommend taking some time to experiment with different ways to see what works for you.

This could take a few weeks or even a few months, and there's undoubtedly going to be an element of trial and error involved, so don't be disheartened if you can't get it to work the first time. Remember, 1 percent better every day is far better than zero percent, so keep trying and keep focusing on what you're doing. Don't be put off by obstacles but instead embrace them as a chance to grow.

Hand in hand with this, I want to clarify that there is no one-size-fits-all solution for everyone. Habit is a very personal thing, and habit tracking is no different. The best method for tracking your habit is the one that works best for you. Aligned with this, here are some considerations you'll need to think about.

Your Tracking Fits Your Personality

It doesn't matter if you know yourself to be hardworking and strict, or you know you go through life a little on the lazy side; you need to embrace the kind of person you are and then work to make your systems—in this case, habit tracking—work in your favor.

This is a very important point that can be applied to all areas of your life. Rather than seeing high-performing individuals you aspire to be and spending your life wishing you were them, focus on what makes you a great individual and what your strengths are. Then, focus on maximizing the outcomes of these while reducing the impact of your weaknesses.

For example, if you're a creative person but not very physically talented from an athletic standpoint, you're not going to aim to become a marathon runner. While the idea is quite nice, it's just not who you are and perhaps not what you're really interested in. In this case, you would aim to find ways to make it easy in your life for you to be creative while keeping your exercise routines enjoyable and straightforward so you keep doing them, rather than just pushing yourself into a routine you hate.

The same applies to habit tracking. If you're the sort of person who loves being organized and getting involved in the data, then you'll choose a very data-rich approach to habit tracking, like creating a spreadsheet. If you're not and you want something fast and easy, you'd pick a simple habit tracking app that gets the job done with no frills attached.

Your Tracking is Appropriate for Your Lifestyle

Someone who lives in a fast-paced environment will have very different demands than someone who lives in a slower, more relaxed environment. Again, if you have time to go into detail with your tracking and it's something you enjoy, then make time for it. If you have a fast-paced, busy life where you don't have much time, then you need a quick and easy solution that won't hold you back.

Choose a Strategy That Makes You Relaxed

This is an essential consideration because the greatest habit tracker for you should put you at ease so that all you have to worry about is practicing your habit, not whether or not you're recording it correctly. More stress will make the tracking process unenjoyable and difficult, and this is the worst approach you could take!

To give you a memorable lowdown, jot down these questions to ask yourself how your habit tracking strategy will serve you and to help you pick the best one from my list in the next section. However, also remember that as you grow and evolve through life, which we all do all the time, you may find yourself changing the strategy you need.

While you may need something quick and easy that you don't want to think about a lot now, in the future, you may place more emphasis on habit tracking and self-development, meaning you'll want to adopt a more detailed approach. Here are your thinking points.

Convenience: How simple and quick is it to gain access to your habit tracking strategy and sign off your day's tasks?

Performance: How are your accomplishments measured, and how does this help you improve?

Flexibility: Can you create your own habit tracker, or do you have to stick to a premade one?

Accountability: Does focusing on your habits make you feel a feeling of responsibility?

Remember that the optimal approach isn't necessarily the one that scores the highest on all criteria, but rather the one that scores at your ideal level.

The Best Habit Tracking Strategies You Can Use Today

Let's get straight into it.

Bullet Journaling

Bullet journaling has rapidly become one of the most popular and most diverse ways of managing life and is a strategy adopted by hundreds of thousands of people around the world.

At its foundation, the art of bullet journaling is about taking a notebook and creating a method for managing your life in a way that uses basic design principles that can be adapted to suit your personal needs.

In other words, you can use bullet journaling strategies for planning, habit tracking, journaling, project managing, diarying, business planning, and so much more.

The basis surrounds the fact that you have a system to plan ahead and remind you of what has to be done, rather than storing all the chores and habits you need to do in your memory and forgetting about them later, or jotting down appointment schedules on random sticky notes and losing track of them later. We've all been there.

Many people like to keep track of their habits in a bullet journal since it is highly adaptable and can be created quickly. Simply get a pen and a notepad, write down the name of your habit and leave some space next to it for recording, and you've got yourself a habit tracker. If you want to run three times a week, you simply write *Run* and then draw three circles representing the times you want to do it.

Once you've done the run, you color in a box, and you're done. That's habit tracking. Since bullet journaling is used to monitor and manage your whole life, it's a book you'll continuously dive into daily, meaning you're always going to be looking at your habits and what you need to do. You're defining what your mind needs to be focusing on by creating new cues and triggers.

More commonly referred to as "BuJo," this is definitely the approach you'll want to take if you're a creative person since it's becoming a bit of an ongoing trend to spend a lot of time attempting to make it appear nice. While having an attractive, colorful, and inspiring habit tracker page in your BuJo is preferable, it's more important to identify what works for you and follow through with this approach.

In other words, worry less about making it pretty and more about having it work. The pretty-looking attempts come later, but this ties in with the whole "making your habit seem attractive" concept. If you enjoy working on your habits, then you're more likely to follow through with them.

Key Thinking Points

- Bullet journals are highly customizable and adaptable. What you put in your tracker is entirely up to you.

- Bullet journals are visually appealing and entertaining, encouraging you to continue tracking.

- There are a variety of templates to pick from, ranging from plain to dramatic.

- The initial tracking template takes a lot of time and work to build.

- You can become engrossed with the aesthetic aspects, devoting most of their time to making their tracker more attractive while spending little time working on their behaviors.

- Carrying the notebook with you may be inconvenient, depending on your lifestyle.

Personal Habit Tracking in a Notebook or Printed Template

If all of the doodles and fillers in a bullet journal seem exhausting, opt for a downloadable template to save time. Using a simple notebook or printed template is a really clear and simple way to track habits that require minimal effort and not a lot of time to set up and get working. This is the very essence of how to-do lists work.

All you need to do is get yourself a notebook and list all the habits you want to introduce or reduce in your life. It might look something like this:

- Get up at six every morning
- Meditate for ten minutes
- Practice yoga for 15 minutes
- Eat a healthy, home-cooked dinner
- Socialize with friends for at least one hour per week
- Write 1,000 words a day
- Go to the gym three times a week

Remember, these habits won't actually be as broad as this. Tying them into everything we spoke about already in the previous chapters, these same habits may look something like this (specific and easy) when you're starting out:

- Put my phone on the other side of the room and get up to turn the 6 a.m. alarm off
- Sit down on my floor for one minute at seven o'clock every morning
- Roll my yoga mat out at 8 o'clock every morning
- Put the ingredients for pasta salad on my worktop at midday
- Text a friend on my first break every day

- Write one sentence
- Drive to the gym car park three times a week as soon as I finish work

Simply list these out in a dedicated notebook and tick them off when they're done. There are plenty of templates out there, especially on the internet, that you can simply print off and use after filling in the blanks of the habits you want to follow through with. All you have to do is choose the one that most appeals to you.

Nice and simple.

The disadvantage of this printed template and notebook strategy is that it involves so little effort that you may overlook it and forget to check it daily. A plain notebook, unlike BuJo, where the act of making up attractive things may thrill you, may easily slip your mind.

If you want to make sure you don't forget to log in your habit on a daily basis, print out templates on a piece of paper and post them somewhere visible in your home or office. Anywhere you have to look at every day, such as the door to your room, the refrigerator, or your desk. Remember, it's all about creating cues that draw your attention to what you're doing and ensure you're able to create new habits.

In line with mastering your environment, keep your notebook and printed templates in sight where you're going to see them all the time to make it so easy to get involved and complete them.

Key Thinking Points

- This strategy is a handier way for those who prefer paper and pen, as it saves them time and effort compared to bullet journaling.

- Because you only have a predefined template to fill in, it's not as versatile as a bullet journal. You may want to make a few notes or adjustments, but you cannot do so due to the restricted space available.

- If you're using printed paper, you might need more than one version: if you only have one at home, you'll have to wait until you go home to track your progress.

- After a few months, storing your tracking papers can be a pain, and you might be tempted to throw away your old tracker. When you try to look back on your development over time, this poses problems because you won't be able to reflect on the progress you've made.

Analog Habit Tracking Methods

The two procedures mentioned above are analog. While many people find these techniques appealing, especially since we live in an age overflowing with digital products and technology, there are clear disadvantages you'll need to overcome, and this will take some trial and error. Remember the key considerations that will make habit tracking work.

You need to make sure your strategy is practical. Your chosen strategy must be easy to carry around, you must have pens with you to fill it out without having to hunt for one, and it must be accessible enough to tick off your habits as soon as possible after completing it. Most people fail at implementing this strategy because there's nothing to remind them to do it. Feeling inspired, they load up their journal into their bag, only for it to be forgotten about when life starts happening.

When people quit using the tracker, they progressively cease tracking the behavior they were tracking, and therefore the habit starts falling by the wayside.

Another problem is that some people don't get much out of tracking. They become bored with the process and don't see the results that would eventually come in the long term fast enough. Only the streaks of their progress are visible to them. To begin with, the prospect of extending that golden streak may be motivating and thrilling, but after people get into the habit and it begins to form, we start to become placid and need something more exciting.

However, in true human fashion, you may start wondering how you can improve, in essence, to get a bigger hit of satisfaction when you continue your streak and stick to your routines. That then raises the question of how you can possibly improve your strategy when they already have a full streak?

This is where modern-day digital solutions come into play.

Digital Tracking Methods

Using an app or digital approach to habit tracking works in the same way that millions of people are obsessed with video games, binge Candy Crush, and spend hours a day on social media. It's attractive to use. You post a photo on Instagram. You get a like. You feel good. You complete a level on Candy Crush. There are some visual fireworks, you go up a level, and you feel like you're making progress.

When you use these same strategies for habit tracking, suddenly, the whole process becomes a lot more engaging and fun. When you get up early, open your phone and tick the habit box for getting up early, you'll get a smiley face, an animated tick, and some experience points, or what reward your preferred app gives.

This may seem silly and insignificant in writing, but when you're actually doing it, it's a very powerful thing to do. If you're doubting, think about how it feels to get a like on your Facebook post, or at least notice how every time you sign on to your most-used social media platform, your eyes will immediately wander to the notifications bell to see how many you've got.

Sorry, you're never going to be able not to see yourself doing that every time you do it from now onwards. Use psychology to make your habits work. That's all there is to it, so with that, let's explore some of the best digital solutions.

Create an Excel or Google Sheets Template

Spreadsheets like Excel or Google Sheets may be a better solution for people who have a penchant for numbers and figures. If you love data, to-do lists, and being organized, this is for you.

The ability to generate statistics distinguishes a spreadsheet from any other habit tracker, especially the analog ones. Whereas those more traditional methods only allow you to track your streaks as you go, these new strategies can offer so much more. Many additional relevant statistics, such as target completion rate, completion time counting, and habit comparison, can be calculated automatically using formulas.

You can either create your own spreadsheet or use one of the many free Google templates that can be effortlessly found online with a quick online search. If you're making your own spreadsheet, I highly recommend checking out the templates anyway because it's a great idea to get inspiration, to see what these sheets are capable of doing, and so you can copy and paste the more complicated yet helpful formulas that they use and those you may be overlooking.

Key Thinking Points

- Spreadsheets can generate many statistics on your behaviors and habits in the form of numbers, percentages, charts, and graphs due to their data-centric nature. This allows you to understand your progress better and develop plans to improve. For example, data may indicate that you should change your goals or eliminate some habits that aren't important to you.

- The display area is quite large and easy to browse. You may quickly run out of space on Excel or Google Sheets, but you can still find the facts you need due to the tab and scrolling system.

- You frequently have to open your laptop to keep track of your progress. While this isn't a significant deal when working on your laptop, consider some of your personal routines, which could cause problems. For example, if you always go on YouTube and watch videos every time you open your laptop, will this be a problem when you open your computer to note your habits?

- You may need to ask yourself whether you're sure you want to open your laptop, which is a representation of your frantic work life, if you want to build a morning routine dedicated to personal well-being—waking up early, exercising, and meditating?

- It can be challenging to browse through your spreadsheet at times. Those are the times when you wish to sync data on your smartphone and use the Google Sheets mobile app, only to discover how difficult it is to locate and change the cell you require. Alternatively, you may simply reach December in your Excel habit tracker, requiring you to scroll rightward indefinitely until you can check off your habit.

- There are few cues you can set up to help you stick with the tracking habit. You will need to do something like stick a Post-it Note to your computer or create a phone alarm that will prompt you to fill out what you're doing. As with all these strategies, building habits is difficult because life always gets in the way. Having a string of hectic days will certainly cause you to lose track of your habit tracker and, as a result, your habit.

Use a Habit Tracking App

This final solution is one of my personal favorites. While I used to use these habit-tracking apps as an attempt to get better, once I started using them alongside everything else we've spoken about in this book, this is when everything really started to fall into place.

You will need to use a habit-tracking mobile app if you want the best help, the best reward system, the best motivation, and the automation of your cues and triggers.

In short, a habit monitoring software can accomplish everything a spreadsheet habit tracker can. Out of the four methods stated, this one has the distinction of mastering the art of simplicity.

Many developers are attempting to make it as easy as possible to track habits and get the most out of the experience with the least amount of effort. This means sending you notifications to remind you to clock in and register what you're doing. This means offering graphical, visual rewards that congratulate you on your progress and keep you going. It means making it easy to check in at any time because, let's face it, who doesn't have their phone on them at all hours of the day?

Since there are so many great apps out there, you will need to do a bit of trial and error to make sure you're using one that works for you, but don't believe for a second that downloading and trailing a load of new tracking habits is adequate progress. I fell into this trap multiple times, thinking that downloading an app was enough hard work to develop my behaviors. It's not. Developing behaviors is working on developing behaviors. This is just another trick of the mind trying to find the easy justified approach.

When choosing an app, you're going to want to look at features like the ability to view your streak as well as your progress toward daily, weekly, and monthly objectives. Extra features like adding notes to the end of every habit you tick off can also be beneficial when reflecting on your progress.

Key Thinking Points

- Habit tracking apps make it incredibly easy to track your habits and behaviors in a satisfying, complete, and visual way that's dramatically rewarding.

- You can automate so many aspects of your process, set up automate cues via notifications, and literally get instant feedback on your actions in a single tap.

- Tons of data can be given to you automatically, which is amazing when it comes to reflecting on how much progress you're making.

- It's very easy to get caught up in the process of trying new apps and exploring new ways of doing things and to mistake this as being progress in itself.

- May require a learning curve to learn how to use the habit.

- You may already have some bad habits linked with using your phone, such as picking it up to browse through social media or watch videos, habits you may fall back into or reinforce because you're going on your phone or tablet.

While these are all great solutions in their own way, at the end of the day, it's all about finding what works for you, so don't be afraid to give them all a go, do your research, and figure out the way you want to move forward, all without feeling disheartened if you have to try more than one thing.

Chapter Eight - The Power of Reflection

"Without reflection, we go blindly on our way." ~ Margaret J. Wheatley

As we start drawing to a close on this book, we've reached a stage where you basically know everything you need to know about bringing new habits in your life and how to become the version of yourself that you want to be.

So far, you've learned about choosing your habits, mastering your mindset, strategies to make developing these habits easy, taking control of your environment, and so on, but this misses out on one crucial aspect, which is what we're going to be focusing on in this chapter. As you've guessed from the chapter title, I'm talking about reflection.

Whether or not you want to hear this, the processing of mastering your habits is not one where there is a set end goal. Your life is constantly changing and ever-evolving, and this means your habits are also going to be evolving with you. A habit serving you well today is fantastic, but you need to change things up if it doesn't serve you in five years. That's right, there are actually downsides to forming new, positive habits, problems that you'll need to be aware of.

The Dark Side of Forming Positive Habits

This is a downside that can be summed up in a single word.

Complacency.

Let's say you're working on building the habit of going to the gym. You start off small and master the art of showing up. You do some runs, do some weights, do some swimming, maybe a class or two, and it's all going smoothly. You're doing really well, and a year or so passes, and you've successfully integrated the habit of going to the gym into your life.

Now that the habit is formed, you just don't think about it, which is great for keeping fit and healthy but bad for progress. Because you've signed the habit off in your mind as complete, you're keeping yourself where you are, which creates several problems. Most notably, you risk getting bored with the activity, whereas more short-term pleasures and bad habits will start to kick in, and you'll stop yourself from becoming the best version of yourself possible.

I use going to the gym because it's such a clear example of this. If you go to the gym and run one kilometer every time you go, if you've never really been the sort of person to run, you're going to see some big benefits to your health and fitness levels. However, as time goes on, you'll be able to run a kilometer like it's nothing, and your curve of progress will flatten out. In other words, you won't actually be gaining any more benefits.

After a few weeks of running one kilometer, the next step is to move up to two kilometers, then three, then five, then ten, and so on. There will obviously be a point where you peak. You might get to ten kilometers and think that you're happy here as a way of staying fit and healthy, and you're always getting the benefits that balance with the rest of your lifestyle, such as how much food you eat and how much time you're able to spend at the gym.

However, there is always a growth period and room to improve, but getting comfortable in your habits can prevent you from doing this if you're not careful and unaware of what you're doing. Of course, some habits don't need this level of attention. When it comes to showering and brushing your teeth, as long as you're doing it to a "good enough" standard, there's no problem. You don't need to be perfect every time you brush your teeth, but when writing or starting a business or being a partner, growth needs to happen.

This is why reflection is so important.

Reflection is basically the act of seeing where you are, taking stock of the habits you're working on, and then analyzing whether you need to keep working on them, improve them, adjust them, drop them, or tweak them. Perhaps you have a habit of getting up early, but you're still finding it hard to follow through.

You could try brute-forcing it and just carrying on how you are and hope that one day everything is going to click into place and you'll suddenly just be waking up early without thinking, or you can reflect on what you're doing and be proactive in looking for ways to improve or grow. Some of your solutions to this specific problem could be something like:

- Moving your alarm to the other side of the room, so you have to get up to turn it off
- Going to bed earlier
- Having a reduced screens policy before bed
- Going for an evening run or walk to tire yourself out
- Eating dinner earlier and not snacking afterward
- Only use your bedroom for sleeping and relaxing

You're not going to get these kinds of insights into the actions you're taking unless you take the time to sit down and reflect on what you're doing, and this is what we're talking about in this next section as we explore some of the best ways to self reflect.

Choose When You Reflect

Start by choosing when you want to reflect, so you're taking the thinking out of the process, making it easier and reducing any friction you encounter. The more specific you are, the better. If you say, "I'm going to reflect on my week on Sunday," when on Sunday? The chances are you'll keep pushing it to later and later in the day until the day is over and you've missed the opportunity.

Instead, say I will reflect on my week every Sunday night at 7 p.m. for 20 minutes. Then, just like every other habit in your life, you need to set everything up for this to happen as seamlessly as possible. This means keeping your diary and a pen out on a table, or your laptop open, in a place where you're going to see it at this time and will develop the cue to reflect.

You could reflect daily in your diary, schedule a weekly check-in with yourself, or give yourself a monthly review.

Personally, I write a diary entry every day, which is just a simple lowdown of everything I did that day, describing how I felt, noting anything I went through down, and basically summarizing the day. I then do a detailed review of the week every Sunday night where I talk about what I excelled at during the week, what I could improve on, and what I'm happy with. I also set myself targets for the next week.

Then every first of the month, I do a habits review where I check in with my process, including the reflection process, and see what I'm doing right, what I'm doing wrong, see what's serving me and not serving me, and see what improvements I can genuinely make.

For example, last month, I focused a lot on my business. I was working on hitting my sales figures, replying to clients fast, dealing with queries more effectively, and figuring out how to manage my time better. However, during my monthly evaluation, I realized I was spending less time with my family than I would have liked to, so I dialed things back a little to figure out how I can be more balanced.

Had I not reflected during this time, I could have ended up going down a much more challenging path.

Ask Yourself Questions

One of the best ways to reflect is to ask yourself questions that will steer your direction of thinking. The questions you ask will determine what you focus on, so make sure you're asking yourself the right questions. Some examples of these could be questions like:

- What habits did I really excel at performing this week?
- What could I do to improve?
- Am I happy or satisfied with the progress and changes I'm making?
- Is there anything about the process I dislike?
- How did I feel today?

Ask these questions and answer as honestly as possible so you know exactly where you're heading and what's going on. This will give your reflections direction and will help you to easily identify where you're at now and where you want to go next.

Choose Your Method

How you reflect on yourself and your life is also an important decision you'll want to make, and there are surprisingly a few methods or strategies to think about.

You could sit down and write in your journal. I use a diary app on my Macbook because I find typing is easier than writing by hand.

You may wish to go for a walk and make notes. You might like to record voice notes or just bullet point the things you are going on. You may like to write essays, articles, or entire paragraphs on what's going on. You could record videos. You could incorporate meditation into your routine.

Even just talking to yourself out loud as you go about your home or go for a walk in nature (probably avoid talking to yourself in a built-up, public place) is a form of reflection, so try different methods out and see what works for you. Don't be afraid to get creative!

Check in with Your Moods

If you're not a fan of writing everything down, or you don't have time just yet, then simply getting into the habit of checking in with your mood every day can be a great way to see how you feel and monitor your progress.

I started out using this method when full-on habit tracking wasn't working for me, and it worked wonders and helped me learn how to connect and understand myself. I used an app specifically for this, but you can use a calendar or even a simple bit of paper. The app sent a notification every day that I opened and simply picked out on a scale of one to six how I was feeling, six being extremely happy and one being extremely sad.

Over time, I was able to see how happy, sad, angry, bored, lonely, and so on I was feeling. Then, when I linked what I was doing within my days that made me feel this way, I started making changes to make myself feel better and start growing as an individual.

Chapter Summary

Once you start introducing the act of reflection into your life, everything changes. It's so easy for the mind to get distracted and to only remember certain aspects of your life, usually in a distorted way that doesn't show you the whole story of a situation. Reflection changes this by giving you the hard facts, and by writing them down and making a record of them, you'll be able to reflect on your life, eventually across the span of years.

If you start reflecting now, you'll create the opportunity to look back on your life and see just how far you've come, and this is something that can change the way you see yourself and your life. Imagine if you had kept a diary every day of your life as a child up until now and how much insight you would get being able to look back on your thoughts and feelings at the time to see what journey you've been on accurately.

This ability to gain insight is essential if you want to become the best version of yourself, which I'm assuming you do since you're reading this book!

Final Thoughts

And so, we come to the end of our journey, or should I say the beginning of the rest of your life? At this point, we've covered literally everything you need to know that will create a solid foundation of new habit creation in your life and everything you need to know when it comes to creating systems and routines that work for you.

Just as the title says, there is literally no need to rely on outdated beliefs that you need willpower, motivation, or discipline to succeed. Sure, they have their own roles to play, and you will need to rely on them from time to time, but they don't make up the core of what you're trying to do. Solid, critical thinking, an open mindset, and the right tools are what you're going to need.

I know I've said this throughout the book, but since this is the last time we'll be speaking, for now, let's visit it one last time. You're a human being. You're going to aim big, and you're not going to get there the first time. You're statistically proven to relapse and fall back into your old ways of living life, and that's okay. There's literally nothing wrong with that. In fact, it's essential because it's all part of the journey.

Aim for 1 percent better every day, not some radical, spiritual enlightenment-styled shift that will happen overnight. That doesn't work. It's a rare chance that will happen. Just take baby steps and make the process easy for yourself. When you think about it, why would you ever put yourself in a position where you're trying to make things hard or brute force things for yourself?

What's the point? Make things easy and genuinely help yourself on your journey. Once you've mastered the basics in this way, you'll have the mental and physical capacity to do even more in your life. Whether you're starting that business, that family, writing that book, or running that marathon, you can devote your energy to these areas of your life rather than constantly battling yourself and fighting against your own neural biology. There are different ways to go, but I believe in you and that you've got what it takes to make it work.

Remember, life is an adventure, and this whole process should be treated as such. You've crossed paths with this book as a map to somewhere unknown. The X that marks the spot is rumored to be the best version of yourself, so are you going to stay in your small humble village, or are you going to get out there, do some quests, have some adventures, make some memories, and see what life is really all about?

It's a choice completely in your own hands.

For now, that's all from me, but as one final request, if you did get anything out of this book, loved parts of it, or had some notes you wanted to share, don't hesitate to leave a review on the site where you purchased this book in the first place.

I read every single review that is posted on all my books because I want to hear what you've got to say and aim to become the very best writer I can be, and your feedback is a massive part of that journey. Don't be afraid to share what you think, and I look forward to hearing from you!

Now, put this book down and get out there and start making things happen! I just know it's going to be beautiful.

References

Daily, T. A. (2016, January 25). 7 Reasons Why It Is Important to Form Good Habits and How to Do It. The Alternative Daily. https://www.thealternativedaily.com/the-importance-of-good-habits/

Free, A. P. T. |. (2021, March 21). 5 Benefits of Developing the Right Habits. Productive and Free. https://www.productiveandfree.com/blog/benefits-of-habits

G., D. (2021, March 26). 67+ Revealing Smartphone Statistics for 2021. TechJury. https://techjury.net/blog/smartphone-usage-statistics/

Spajic, D. J. (2020, December 14). How Much Time Does the Average Person Spend on Their Phone? KommandoTech. https://kommandotech.com/statistics/how-much-time-does-the-average-person-spend-on-their-phone/

("Habit Tracking Methods - Which One Is For You?", 2021)

Zuckerman, A. (2020, May 19). 32 Happiness Statistics: 2020/2021 Data, Trends & Facts. CompareCamp.Com. https://comparecamp.com/happiness-statistics/

Ortiz-Ospina, E. (2013, May 14). Happiness and Life Satisfaction. Our World in Data. https://ourworldindata.org/happiness-and-life-satisfaction

habit. (2021). The Merriam-Webster.Com Dictionary. https://www.merriam-webster.com/dictionary/habit

How the brain controls our habits. (2012, October 30). MIT News | Massachusetts Institute of Technology. https://news.mit.edu/2012/understanding-how-brains-control-our-habits-1029

Clear, J. (2021). Atomic Habits. Random House. https://www.amazon.co.uk/Atomic-Habits-Proven-Build Break/dp/B07J1XQSNK/ref=sr_1_1?dchild=1&keywords=atomic+habits&qid=1623768231&sr=8-1

Mcleod, S. (2018, October 8). Pavlov's Dogs. Simply Psychology. https://www.simplypsychology.org/pavlov.html

Also by James W. Williams

- How to Read People Like a Book: A Guide to Speed-Reading People, Understand Body Language and Emotions, Decode Intentions, and Connect Effortlessly
- Communication Skills Training: How to Talk to Anyone, Connect Effortlessly, Develop Charisma, and Become a People Person
- How to Make People Laugh: Develop Confidence and Charisma, Master Improv Comedy, and Be More Witty with Anyone, Anytime, Anywhere
- Digital Minimalism in Everyday Life: Overcome Technology Addiction, Declutter Your Mind, and Reclaim Your Freedom
- Self-discipline Mastery: Develop Navy Seal Mental Toughness, Unbreakable Grit, Spartan Mindset, Build Good Habits, and Increase Your Productivity
- How to Make People Like You: 19 Science-Based Methods to Increase Your Charisma, Spark Attraction, Win Friends, and Connect Effortlessly
- How to Make People Do What You Want: Methods of Subtle Psychology to Read People, Persuade, and Influence Human Behavior

- How to Talk to Anyone About Anything: Improve Your Social Skills, Master Small Talk, Connect Effortlessly, and Make Real Friends
- Listening Skills Training: How to Truly Listen, Understand, and Validate for Better and Deeper Connections
- How to Spot a Liar: A Practical Guide to Speed Read People, Decipher Body Language, Detect Deception, and Get to The Truth